Total Quality Management

A Comprehensive Strategy Toward the Implementation of an Effective and Efficient Healthcare Delivery System in Africa

John Ngosong Morfaw

UNIVERSITY PRESS OF AMERICA,® INC.

Lanham • Boulder • New York • Toronto • Oxford

Copyright © 2006 by
University Press of America,® Inc.
4501 Forbes Boulevard
Suite 200
Lanham, Maryland 20706
UPA Acquisitions Department (301) 459-3366

PO Box 317
Oxford
OX2 9RU, UK

Library of Congress Control Number: 2005937429
ISBN 13: 978-0-7618-3293-5 (paperback : alk. ppr.)
ISBN 10: 0-7618-3293-9 (paperback : alk. ppr.)

$\otimes^{TM}$ The paper used in this publication meets the minimum
requirements of American National Standard for Information
Sciences—Permanence of Paper for Printed Library Materials,
ANSI Z39.48—1992

This book is dedicated to my beloved late father, grandfather, guardian and friend, Papa WuafuawTanyinguh of Fonge Village, my late grandmother, mother, guardian and friend, Mama Esther Nkengafaih Wuafuaw and my late grand uncle, His Royal Highness ChiefAlexander Ngrossong Fuawenje-ih of Fonge Village, and My children-Nkengafac Morfaw and Muyang Mor-faw (The Mor Sisters)

CONTENTS

Charts and Tables

Preface

Total Quality Management (TQM) is achieved through employee empowerment in decision making, the use of facilitated teams in the organization, individual responsibility for products and services and a strong customer service orientation, working from a set of values envisioning a mission, maintaining commitment, sustaining motivation, prioritizing tasks, cooperating with others, communicating effectively and seeking to continuously learn and grow.

In Africa, the health care industry is plagued by a catalogue of social, economic, political, cultural, structural and organizational problems, needing some reform, restructuring, reorganization and reengineering through the introduction and implementation of quality management concepts such as Total Quality Management (TQM). This will involve intensive and extensive education and training of all medical support personnel on effective and efficient as well as qualitative health service delivery to communities. This will also require reorganization and restructuring of existing medical institutions, policy and system changes on major healthcare delivery systems in the continent.

This book focuses on basic quality improvement tools such as process flow analysis, cost-benefit and cost-effectiveness analysis, quality organizational structures, systems analysis, organizational behavior and team building which help to analyze and evaluate various quality management processes.

The implementation of quality improvement processes continues to grow in organizations since most great projects have been accomplished through effective and efficient and management of the processes. The realization of giant space projects, manufacture of airplanes, cars, computers are all successful through configuration management in the assembly line and total quality management in the implementation.

A couple of books have been written on Total Quality Management in businesses but few have been written on it in the healthcare industry and with specific focus on the African continent. What is needed now is a book that addresses a comprehensive approach to the accomplishment of quality service delivery to customers.

This book outlines the philosophy, principles, goals and objectives of the Total Quality Management concept and analyzes and evaluates a couple of programs involved in quality assurance programs in the healthcare industry in Africa. It ends up with a comprehensive strategic implementation plan for a typical Total Quality Management process in an organization.

This book is intended to be a textbook for undergraduate and graduate students in business schools, medical schools and allied health professions. It is also intended for use in vocational and other trade centers.

The book is also intended as a consulting manual for professional consultants in project management, quality assurance, quality improvement and general management, health research institutions, hospitals and clinics, health insurance companies, small and large-scale businesses, Non-Governmental and other international organizations involved in healthcare services around the world.

Although the book is focused on the implementation of the Total Quality Management concept in the African healthcare industry, it is also a very valuable manual for students, scholars, researchers, consultants and other professionals undertaking comparative studies on healthcare issues in Europe, Asia, South America, the Caribbean and the United States. Exploiting the content of this book will enable the readers to better understand the problems and potentials of the healthcare industry in this continent. It will also enable them to fully understand various activities being undertaking by some international organizations such as the World Health Organization, the World Bank, the Council of Health Services Accreditation of Southern Africa, the United Agency for International Development, The African Medical and Research Foundation, the African Networks for Health Research and Development, the West African Doctors and Healthcare Professionals Network, the African Population and Health Research Center, the African Council for Sustainable Health Development, the Population Council and a host of others involved in various program to ameliorate the health conditions in Africa.

Brookhaven, Pennsylvania, USA   John Ngosong Morfaw
June 2005.

Acknowledgment

My deep appreciation for this project goes to Dr. Janice M. Charlton of Penn State University, Great Valley-Malvern, Pennsylvania for proof reading and editing the book. Special love goes to my dear sweet wife, Mrs. Pamela Asangong-Morfaw for contributing ideas and proof-reading the manuscript as well as her relentless support towards the accomplishment of this project.

Many thanks also go to the World Health Organization Corporate Office in Geneva, Switzerland, and the United Nations International Children's Emergency Fund for authorizing me to use their material and relevant statistics in the book. I also expressed heartfelt thanks to Max Wideman of Canada for permitting me to exploit his Dictionary of Project Management Terms.

Acronyms

*TQM	Total Quality Management
* QC	Quality Control
*CQI	Continuous Quality Improvement
*QA	Quality Assurance
*TQC	Total Quality Control
*ISO	International Organization for Standardization
*IOM	International Organization for Migration
*COHSASA	Council of Health Service Accreditation of Southern Africa
*NGO	Non-Governmental Organization
*WHO	World Health Organization
*UN	United Nations
*IMF	International Monetary Fund
*UNDP	United Nations Development Program
*UNPF	United Nations Population Fund
*USAID	United States Agency for International Development
*JHPIEGO	John Hopkins Program for International Education in Gynecology and Obstetrics
* ISQua	International Society for Quality in Health Care Inc.
*QAP	Quality Assurance Project
*WTO	World Trade Organization
*ILO	International Labor Organization
*SANSA	South African Network for Skills Abroad
*ANSI	American National Standards Institute
*CAFS	Center for African Family Studies
*AMREF	The African Medical and Research Foundation
*SAP	Structural Adjustment Program

*ACOSHED	African Council for Sustainable Health Development
*APHRC	African Population and Health Research Center
*WADN	West African Doctors and Healthcare Professionals Network
*AfHR	The African Health Research Forum
*AFRO-NETS	African Networks for Health Research and Development 000

Chapter One

1:00- DEFINITION OF TOTAL QUALITY MANAGEMENT

Total Quality Management (TQM) is a philosophy of total organizational involvement in improving all aspects of the quality of product or service provided by the organization. It is also referred to as *Total Quality Control (TQC), Total Quality Leadership (TQL), Integrated Quality Management (IQM), Continuous Quality Improvement (CQI), Quality Management Science (QMS), Industrial Quality Management (IQM) or Configuration Management (CM)* depending on the philosophy, goals and objectives of the industry or organization where it is being implemented. This concept is achieved through employee empowerment in decision making, the use of facilitated teams in the organization, individual responsibility for products and services, a strong customer service orientation, working from a set of values envisioning a mission, maintaining commitment, sustaining motivation, prioritizing tasks, cooperating and collaborating with others, communicating effectively and efficiently and seeking to continuously learn and grow.

The first application of management theory took place in non-profits and governmental agencies and the first conscious and systematic application of this management principle was in the reorganization of the US Army in 1901. The identification of management with business began with the Great Depression of 1929and continued throughout the Second World War, and became more intensified after the war during the period of reconstruction.

The concept of Total Quality Management has grown out of the work of several individuals who have studied and developed models for personal and organizational effectiveness and improvements. These individuals include Dr. W. Edwards Deming, Stephen Covey, Joseph Juran and Philip Crosby who

1

professed that unfaltering commitment by all is essential for an effective and efficient implementation of an organization's philosophy, goals and objectives. Isolated examples of excellence are not the goal, but system-wide quality. This requires providing training to everyone, not only in his or her areas of expertise, but also in the areas of personal responsibility, leadership and improvement progress. These individuals were later sent to Japan by the US State Department to help in the reconstruction of the Japanese economy badly devastated by the bombings during the war. The Japanese easily embraced the TQM concept and it quickly revolutionized their economy and that remains one of the greatest turning points in Japanese economic miracle. Throughout its industrial recovery and take-off in the late 1940's and the 1950's, Japanese industries such as Sony, Yamaha, Suzuki, and Toyota etc have all implemented the TQM concept and it has tremendously helped in the enhancement of the quality of its goods and services. Japanese companies now have affiliates and franchises in almost every country around the globe with available experts for customer service and other necessary assistance.

The term Total Quality Management was first introduced in Great Britain in 1983 by the Trade and Industry Department of Margaret Thatcher's government when it launched its quality campaign. It is a proven method of reaching the goal of quality. This is a leadership system that responds to customers while creating and maintaining an organization culture that values involvement and continuous efforts to improve quality. It is a philosophy that includes learning to apply the necessary techniques, tools and viewpoints that allow organizations to keep customers and maintain a positive rewarding work environment for employees.

The underlying principles of Total Quality Management have been stated in many ways, but they include the basic ideas of working from a set of values envisioning a mission, maintaining commitment, sustaining motivation, prioritizing tasks, cooperating with others, communicating effectively, and seeking to continuously learn and grow. By putting these ideas into practice, individuals and organizations achieve significant and readily apparent benefits for themselves and others. The basic concept behind TQM is that it is very expensive to maintain quality by inspections, and much more efficient to build quality products in the first place. As a result, the responsibility for quality is placed with the workers who actually produce the products. Quality control departments are therefore refocused on different responsibilities, such as training employees in quality control, conducting audits of the quality of the company's parts and suppliers, making final test of finished goods and implementing quality control concepts throughout the company. There are many aspects to TQM such as employee empowerment in decision-making, the use of teams in organization, individual responsibility for products or services, and strong customer service orientation.

Total Quality Management is intended to result in the improvement of services and products not by looking at what is produced but by examining the process for root causes of problems, defects and errors. Total Quality Management relies on the development of personally effective individuals committed to a common vision and an emphasis on customer needs and perceptions. It is based on scientific approaches to decision making, using sequential steps to gather and analyze information in an objective manner and monitoring and evaluating processes with data and statistical tools. Another important feature of TQM is the shift in focus from the end product or service to the processes involved. By focusing on how something is done, rather than what is accomplished, quality can be most dramatically impacted, which ultimately results in improved products and services.

TQM is not a simple solution to quality problems or management issues, but it is an effective one. TQM usually demands cultural changes within the organization because it is a different system to be added to the already existing traditional organizational structures and paradigms. Modern corporate management now has to focus on the long-term, market orientation, a participative management culture, process control and a commitment to continuously improve all products and services. These prerequisites all fall within the general category of principles and practices of Total Quality Management (TQM), Total Quality Control (TQC), and Continuous Quality Improvement (CQI). Companies vary in how they describe the TQM environment, for example Texas Instruments describes its comprehensive management model as having five interrelated components: customer first, teamwork, management by fact, excellence, and policy deployment. Hewlett-Packard describes its Total Quality system as including four cornerstones: customer focus, planning, process management, and an improvement cycle. With the adoption of TQM in 1989, the National Society for Professional Engineers (NSPE) with its 250 projects knew that this meant that their organization was customer-focused; process-oriented, and committed to continuous improvement.

While implementation of TQM may yield immediate, visible improvement, the goal is not to quick-fix things but to develop relationships and processes capable of generating and sustaining quality improvement now and in the future. For the 21st century corporate world, social contracts will be essential because they link employees to employer, and because the natural responsibility of employees arise from social contracts based on trust by employers and employees. The employee invests his resources in the organization and the organization owes individuals investment in term of development job experience, education, salary and supportive and conducive environment.

Although the TQM concept has been sweeping across the business world for a couple of decades, it has not yet penetrated the African continent especially the healthcare sector. Actually the African Healthcare industry is experiencing serious managerial, organizational and structural problems requiring the implementation of the TQM strategy in order to improve service delivery. Only a few countries such as South Africa, Namibia, Malawi and Ghana are struggling to implement some quality assurance programs through external help from organizations from Europe and the United States.

1:01-PROBLEM STATEMENT

It is a truism that American and World businesses are undergoing their most profound transformation since the Industrial Revolution. As we strive to get ready for business in the 21st Century and struggle to deal with today's business in the 1990's, we must come to grips with the hard reality that traditional business concepts and philosophies just don't work any more. Basically, everything we know and do is in a state of changing at lightning speed and with drastic and devastating effects. Chaos and instability affect many of our organizations as this process leaves us wondering what the future might hold. Hierarchy, the cultural principle by which we have led and managed business for the past century, no longer seems practical or relevant. Jobs are being eliminated or totally redesigned. A number of companies have come up with a potpourri of programs designed to change the structure of their work places but not their essence—the culture. Downsizing, re-engineering, and restructuring programs have succeeded in altering the employment base and cost structure of our companies, but do not offer a new cultural framework. Programs that focus on organizational effectiveness, empowerment, total quality and self-directed work teams have been powerful tools for change in some companies.

In the African continent, nepotism, mismanagement, corruption, fraud and political instability plague the system, coupled with the lack of financial and material resources and technical know-how. Its healthcare industry has been deeply affected by mounting problems, which need to be addressed, and corrections made. This is further compounded by the brain drain where educated and skilled African professionals leave the continent to developed countries in such of better jobs, career opportunities and improved social and economic life. This has paralyzed the labor sector of most African economies especially the healthcare industry. As a result, service delivery is non-existent in some areas especially the rural communities, and where it exists, it is poorly managed. The Total Quality Management strategy is the best approach at this point to make an effective and efficient change in Africa's healthcare delivery system.

According to WHO Director-ccccsGeneral Dr. Gro Harlem Brundtland, the health and well being of people around the world depend critically on the performance of the health systems that serve them. Yet there is wide variation in performance, even among countries with similar levels of income and health expenditure. It is essential for decision-makers to understand the underlying reasons so that system performance, and hence the health of populations, can be improved. WHO's Director for Global Program on Evidence for Health Policy, Dr Christopher Murray says that although significant progress has been achieved in past decades, virtually all countries are underutilizing the resources that are available to them. This leads to large numbers of preventable deaths and disabilities, unnecessary suffering injustice, inequality and denial of an individual's basic rights to health.

The WHO Report (2000), states that he impact of failures in health systems is most severe on the poor everywhere, who are driven deeper into poverty by lack of financial protection against ill-health. And Dr. Brundtland further states that the poor are treated with less respect, given less choice of service providers and offered lower-quality amenities. The World Health Report concludes that the main failings of many health systems are:

1) Many health ministries focus on the public sector and often disregard the frequently much larger private sector health care.
2) In many countries, some if not most physicians work simultaneously for the public sector and in private practice. This means the public sector ends up subsiding unofficial private practice.
3) Many governments fail to prevent a "black market" in health, where widespread corruption, bribery, " moonlighting" and other legal practices flourish. The black markets, which themselves are caused by malfunctioning health systems, and low income of health workers, further undermine those systems.
4) Many health ministries fail to enforce regulations that they themselves have created or are supposed to implement in the public interest.

Most African countries at varying paces are pursuing health service decentralization. Decentralization of authority, responsibility, and resources for personnel functions is important to achieve effective human resource management and to improve staff performance. However, decentralization itself entails large-scale development of capacity at the local level for health planning, financing, allocation and accounting for resources, and human resources management functions including staff recruitment, payroll and allowance documentation, and maintenance of personnel records. Doctors and nurses who have passed to local level supervision would need to upgrade their skills in epidemiology, planning, and management. Decentralization also entails retraining central-level health staff on their new functions in stewardship, setting and maintaining standards, regulation, and monitoring of health services provided at the local level, thus the need for skills in fields such as health planning, quality assurance, health economics and financing, and health systems management. But even more serious than training itself is the need to set up new systems and procedures to make local health services work. These new structures, new budgeting and reporting mechanisms, and new relationships between the central ministries (health, local government, finance, etc.) on the other hand, and the local government units and peripheral health facilities on the other, are straining the human resources capacities of all parties. With respect to the health, professional, decentralization often brings organizational structures and career paths that may become even more limited unless deliberate efforts are made to break down traditional restrictions on the professional backgrounds required for district management positions. The ongoing decentralization in many Africa countries certainly could be expedited with far greater attention to human resources potential deficits. Based on past African experiences, three key areas usually have been missed or ignored in deliberations about health workers:

- The pragmatic and realistic assessment of the types of health workers most needed, based on a careful analysis of the country's burden of disease rather than an idealized notion of care that is desired,
- The sustainable size of the health workforce, the balance between different types of workers, and underpinning this, the sustainable size of the country's health facility network itself and
- The role of private providers in the country's health system and the interactions and cooperative partnerships that should be established between public and private providers.

To redress the managerial and technical scarcities, organizations often provide technical assistance in areas such as health sector reform strategies, drug management and logistics, district financing, management of critical disease control programs, or program implementation coordination, such as the World Bank project implementation units. Strong government vision, leadership, and management of expatriates is required, otherwise, they may lead the medical professionals to develop systems and approaches that may not be appropriate for long-term sustainability.

Some African countries have shown a degree of success in equalizing the regional distribution of trained. Urban and rural disparities, however, continue to persist and may be getting worse in many African countries. Poor spatial distribution of health workers has always been a problem in the developing world, but this is markedly so in Africa, probably because of its lower level of urbanization. Typical of trained professionals, African doctors and nurses prefer to work in urban hospital setting where professional camaraderie is readily available and promotion is more probable. The availability of urban amenities (good housing, schooling for their children, and leisure) is also an important consideration. Finally, the urban location of most hospitals, where the majority of health workers are concentrated, somehow makes it inevitable that health workers are mostly in cities. Given these factors, it is extremely challenging to attract health workers outside cities.

1:02- JUSTIFICATION OF THE IMPLEMENTATION OF TOTAL QUALITY MANAGEMENT IN THE AFRICAN HEALTHCARE INDUSTRY.

The TQM concept and philosophy is sweeping across the corporate world and has been greatly embraced by some Fortune 500 corporations such as IBM, Coca Cola, Unisys, Mobil, Texaco, and Africa's healthcare industry is not left out. It is therefore very necessary to carry out a study of this nature so as to analyze and evaluate the effects and impact of the implementation of the process on Africa's productivity. This will help to justify the degree of resource utilization, the output and the overall efficiency and effectiveness of the company's operation in the community as well as the problems and potentials created or solved by this process.

This publication is well justified in that one will be able to examine how TQM can change Africa's work culture, its organizational structure, and its programs and activities and its effects and impact on its corporate values. A cost-benefit analysis of TQM programs will help to determine its degree of sustainability and how profitable it is for the continent. This will justify whether it is measurable, acceptable and achievable project to have been undertaken.

Peter Drucker, a great theorist and prolific writer on modern management says these are obsolete assumptions and companies should turn to TQM style of management. He laments that way back; the right way was top-down control-centralization. Today the approach is the team management, which is a TQM model, and considered ideal. Author Drucker further emphasized the importance of management by saying that, "The center of modern society is the managed institution". The managed institution is the society's way of getting things done these days. And Management is the specific tool, the specific function, and the specific instrument, to make institutions capable of producing results.

The African Healthcare industry definitely needs the implementation of new quality management concepts such as the TQM for a more effective and efficient service delivery. This will be a total paradigm shift in the system requiring a lot of cultural, structural, organizational and managerial adjustments, which will affect both the employees and patients. This will require a continuous investment of material, human and financial resources to:

- Examine how the TQM strategy is being implemented and the existing modalities and structures for such implementation.
- Ascertain the effects and impact of TQM on the company's productivity, efficiency and effectiveness.
- Find out the technology employed in the successful implementation of the process by the healthcare systems in Africa,
- Find out the existing training facilities, which facilitates TQM implementation in Africa medical institutions and facilities,
- Carry out a cost-benefit analysis of TQM implementation by various African governments.
- Analyze and evaluate the effects and impact of TQM on the system's values, culture and employee moral.
- Study the contribution of Total Quality Management strategy on Africa's healthcare delivery system.
- Identify possible potentials for growth resulting from TQM process implementation by some African governments.
- Come up with possible solutions for improvement on the identified problems.
- Develop strategic and dynamic recommendations to ameliorate the implementation of TQM process in healthcare facilities.

1:03-ORGANIZATION OF THE BOOK

This book is divided into eight chapters as follows:

Chapter One deals with the introduction to the general principles and concept Total Quality Management and the problem statement. Also discussed in this chapter are the justification of the study, the scope and limitation methodology and the limitations of the study.

Chapter Two deals with the concept of Total Quality Management (TQM), the philosophers or gurus of this concept such as Edward Deming, Joseph Juran and Philip Crosby. The chapter also talks about TQM culture, its basic principles, process techniques and tools, management teams, Quality organizational structures and Quality Improvement process. The chapter also dwells on TQM organizational structure, various teams, panels and their roles and compares traditional and Total Quality Management.

Chapter Three discusses the Total Quality Management Process Improvement techniques such as the Process Flowchart, various statistical and management tools.

Chapter four focuses on the Quality organizational Structure as a cardinal instrument in the successful implementation of a management process. Various departments and divisions of the structure and their roles are discussed. It also compares Total Quality management and the paradigm Shift and the International organization for Standardization (ISO) series of standards.

Chapter Five deals with the status of healthcare and human resources crisis in the African continent.

Chapter Six analyzes and evaluates various programs in place in African countries dealing with quality assurance and improvement such as Advance Africa, the Quality Assurance Project (QAP), the John Hopkins University Program in Africa (JHPIEGO), The Council of Health Service Accreditation of Southern Africa (COHSASA), The Population Council, The Center for African Family Services (CAFS), the African Medical and Research Foundation (AMREF), and the activities of the World Health Organization (WHO) in Africa, the World bank, the African Networks for Health Research and development, the African health Research Forum, the West African Doctors and Healthcare Professionals Network, the African Population and Health Research Center and the African Council for Sustainable Health Development.

Chapter Seven examines various healthcare systems around the world and elaborates on healthcare systems of some African countries such as South Africa, Nigeria, Cameroon, Ghana, Tanzania, Kenya, Ethiopia and Botswana. This chapter also analyses the design of an effective and efficient healthcare system.

Chapter eight focuses on the implementation of the Total Quality Management concept in an organization, the development and implementation of a corporate strategic plan and the TQM training modalities and process.

Chapter Two

2:00- FUNDAMENTALS OF TOTAL QUALITY MANAGEMENT

TQM has its roots in America and many of its elements are rooted in theories and practices of management that were developed in the USA. Problems arise primarily from imperfect processes, not from imperfect people. Industrial experience has shown that 85% of all problems are process problems that are solvable by managers, with the remaining 15% being problems requiring the action and improvement of performance of individual workers. This principle is popularly known as the "85/15 Principle". Thus quality problems are primarily management problems because only management has the power to change work processes. Schmidt and Finnigan (1992) suggest that TQM's roots include: -

- Scientific Management—Finding the best way to do a job,
- Group Dynamics—Enlisting and organizing the power of group experience,
- Training and Development—Investing in human capital,
- Achievement Motivation—People getting satisfaction from accomplishment,
- Employee Involvement—Workers should have some influence in the organization,
- Socio-Technical System—Organizations operating as open systems,
- Organization Development—Helping organizations to learn and change
- Corporate Culture—Beliefs, myths, and values that guide the behavior of people throughout the organization,
- The New Leadership Theory—Inspiring and empowering others to act,
- The Linking-Pin Concept of Organization—Creating cross-functional teams,

- Strategic Planning—Determining where to take the organization and how and when to get there.

According to William P. Anthony t al (1996) TQM is a strategic, integrated system of management for achieving satisfaction that involves managers and employees and uses quantitative methods to continuously improve quality. This concept continued to sweep across corporate America in the 1970's. This led to a mad rush of small and medium sized companies into it, as well as giant companies, such as General Motors, ICI, and British Petroleum. Michele L. Bechtell (1995) outlines some basic principles, which describe some basic practices associated with the school of Total Quality Management such as:

- Aligning the organization's goals with change in the environment'
- Focusing on the vital few strategic traps,
- Working with others to develop plan to close the gaps,
- Specifying the methods and measures to achieve the strategic objectives,
- Making visible the causes and effective linkages among local plans and continuously improving the planning process.

Bechtel, Michele (1995), states that the standardized problem-solving methodology from the school of Total Quality Management is a logical common sense method of solving any type of problem, and that the problem-solving process provides a road map to help senior management and other employees solve problems during the improvement journey. The author outlines the problem-solving steps as follows:

1) Select the issue.
2) Search for data to describe the situation
3) Analyze the data/facts to obtain root causes of the performance gap
4) Select a solution
5) Conduct a pilot test
6) Evaluate performance
7) Standardize, reflect and repeat the entire process

The method, according to the author, provides a record of the decision making process. William Bridges (1995) states that today's organizations are being transformed from a structure built out of job to s field out of work needing to be done. The author concludes that all these fall within the general category of principle and practices described by "Total Quality Management" (TQM), and "Total Quality Control" (TQC), and "Continuous Quality Improvement" (CQI). According to John MacDonald (1998) the concept of Total Quality Management was not totally new to evolutionary companies, since

most had been focusing on quality goods and services. This point is exempli-
fied by the approach of 3M and General Motors. Total Quality Management
was profoundly influenced by developments in Japan, but it is not a phenom-
enon that can be bonded "Made in Japan." According to Dennis Waitley
(1995) the new employee paradigms conforms to the concept of principles of
Total Quality Management and are clearly stated as: -

- Autonomy and Empowerment, which means minimal supervision and max-
  imum Training,
- Meaningful Work—which should be environmentally safe with a mission
  to help Society,
- Career Path—employees want opportunities to grow and move up the ladder,
- Incentives—employees need compensation based on performance stan-
  dards,
- Flexible Schedule—consideration of family and cultural pursuits,
- Team Leader—able to be a standout while remaining a team player.

In asserting the significance of TQM, Paul Neblock (1992) says that TQM
is a structured program an organization uses to continually improve its operation; Management totally rethinks how the organization is run and restruc-
tures it for maximum effectiveness. Neblock further state that the cultural
changes required by TQM empowers staff members so that they have more
say on how decisions are made, thereby reducing turnover and fostering the
teamwork that is a crucial element of a successful TQM program. Neblock,
(1992) asserts that the heart of TQM is meeting the needs of customers who
are both external and internal.

Collaboration is the premier candidate to replace hierarchy as the organizing principle for leading and managing the 21st century workplace, Edward
E, Marshall (1995). He further reasserted the importance of this principle by
outlining seven core values, which add up to its significance and continue to
surface again and again as the basis for effective work relationships: -

1) Respect for people, Honor and Integrity,
2) Ownership,
3) Alignment,
4) Consensus
5) Full responsibility,
6) Trust-based relationships, and
7) Recognition and growth.

Edward E. Marshall further outlined some of the benefits of Collaboration
such as:

- Faster decision-making,
- Reduction in cycle time,
- Increased productivity,
- Increased return on investment,
- Increased span of control,
- More responsibility and accountability,
- Reduction in conflict,
- Higher quality and
- Customer-driven decisions.

He outlines some core components of a successful collaborative Total Quality Management team such as:

1) Collaborative Culture,
2) Collaborative Leadership,
3) Strategic Vision,
4) Collaborative Team Processes, and
5) Collaborative Culture.

The icon of modern management, Peter F. Drucker (1998) lamented on the need for change into modern Organizational Management, a Total Quality Management style by justifying through seven underlying assumptions about organizations that are out of date which state that:

1) There is only one right way to organize a business,
2) The principles of management apply to business organizations,
3) There is a single way to manage people,
4) Technologies, markets and end users are fixed and rarely overlap,
5) Management's scope is legally defined as applying only to an organization's assets and employees,
6) Management's job is to run the business rather than to concentrate on what is happening outside the business.

In the healthcare industry quality improvement processes vary from one department to the next from one profession to the other. For example physicians might view a healthcare organization as a provider of processes for patient examination, patient testing, patient diagnosis and treatment. Healthcare administrators might view the activities in terms of admitting patients, tracking patient services, discharging patients and billing for the cost of services. Laboratory analysts might view their work as processes for acquiring samples, analyzing samples, performing quality control and releasing patient test results.

The effective and efficient implementation of the Total Management strategy in an organization depends on some basic and fundamental activities and processes. These all help to define the quantity and quality of work and the various protocol and ethical standards required in the implementation process. Some of these activities are the Goals, Objectives and Philosophy, Quality Assessment, Quality Control, Quality Processes and Processing. The relationship among these processes is diagrammatically illustrated as this:

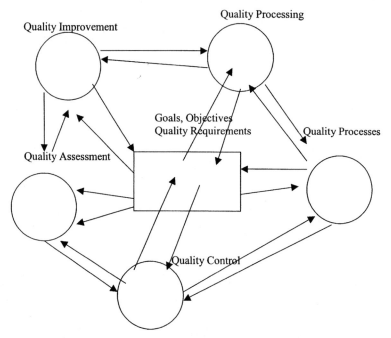

Chart 2:01.   Basic Total Quality Management Framework

Total Quality Management is ineffective and inefficient without these processes and relationships.

2:01-BASIC TENETS OF TOTAL QUALITY MANAGEMENT

Total Quality Management has some basic tenets, which continue to influence its implementation across corporations such as: -

2:02:01- Systematic Approach to Problems:

Problems or opportunities for improvement are dealt with in many different ways, but quality organizations use a systematic, databased approach to avoid mistakes and to eliminate short-term fixes that result in greater problems in the future—TQM is not a "quick fix."

2:02:02- Focus on Action:

Posters, T-shirts and other promotional items do not on their own improve quality. Without claims of quality, these promotional items become nothing more than great jobs. TQM is not conveyed by slogans, but through the actions of leaders and all employees.

2:02:03- Accepted and Practiced by All:

In order to work, TQM must be integrated into the daily operations of the entire organization. All must reach the philosophies of TQM because it is not a departmental or specialist function.

2:02:04- Change in Culture:

TQM involves many changes in individual thinking and organizational philosophy, and this does not happen overnight.

2:02:05- Commitment to Top Leadership:

Without commitment from the top, TQM simply will not work, because its success depends on good leadership. Leaders cannot delegate responsibility for Total Quality

2:02:06- Continuous, Systematic Improvement:

TQM affects the basic operational systems of an organization and provides for continuous improvement of these and all other day-to-day operations.

2:02:07- Long-Term Commitment:

TQM is infinite, a long-term project reading continuous efforts to improve systems and adjust to the changing demand of customers.

2:02-THE GURUS OF TOTAL QUALITY MANAGEMENT

Today, there are dozens of organizations practicing quality maintenance and improvement under different names and with varied approaches. There are, however, three pioneers of Total Quality Management on whose thesis and concepts we depend on today. They are W. Edwards Deming, Joseph M. Juran and Philip B. Crosby. Corporations such as AT&T, Chrysler, Dow Chemical, Ford, General Motors, IBM and Xerox originally based their quality systems on the philosophies delivered by these three innovators.

2:02: 01-W. Edward Deming's 14 Points for Quality Improvement

Deming is credited with much of Japan's industrial escalation and centralization after World Ward II. While working for the US State Department in the late 1940's, he was sent to Japan, where he taught his methods. Along with his 14 points, Deming's philosophy relies heavily on statistical process control. Deming believes that the majority of quality problems are caused by ineffective management practices. His 14 points for quality improvement are: -

1) Create and publish to all employees a statement of the aims and purposes of the company or other organization. The management must demonstrate constantly their commitment to this statement.
2) Learn the new philosophy, top management and everybody.
3) Understand the purpose of inspection, for improvement of processes and reduction of costs.
4) End the practice of awarding business on the basis of price tag alone.
5) Improve constantly and forever the system of production & service.
6) Institute training of Personnel.
7) Teach and institute leadership
8) Drive out fear. Create trust. Create a climate for innovation.
9) Optimize toward the aims and purposes of the company, the efforts of teams, groups and staff areas.
10) Eliminate exhortations for the workforce.
11a. Eliminate numerical quotas for production, instead learn and institute methods for improvement.
11b. Eliminate M.B.O. Instead, learn the capabilities of processes, and how to improve them.
12. Remove barriers that rob people of pride of workmanship.
13. Encourage education and self-improvement for everyone.
14) Take action to accomplish the transformation.

2:02: 02-Joseph M. Juran's 10 Steps to Quality Improvement

Juran, like Deming, was instrumental in helping Japan rebuild its industrial base following World War II. His work is greatly concerned with eliminating production flows, and, he focuses more on improvements within the "parts" of Joseph M. Juran's 10 steps to Quality Improvement are as follows:

1) Build awareness of the need and opportunity for improvement.
2) Set goals for improvement.
3) Organize to reach the goals.
4) Provide training.
5) Carry out projects to solve problems.
6) Report progress.
7) Give recognition.
8) Community results.
9) Keep score.
10) Maintain momentum by making annual improvement part of the regular system and processes of the company.

An organization.

2:03: 03-Philip B. Crosby's 14 Steps to Quality Improvement

Crosby believes that quality is measurable and is the responsibility of everyone in an organization. He is very "bottom-line" oriented and believes that quality is the key to an organization's financial success. Philip B. Crosby's 14 steps to Quality Improvement are as follows:

1) Make it clear that leadership is committed to quality.
2) Form quality improvement teams with representatives from each department.
3) Determine where current and potential quality problems lie.
4) Evaluate the quality awareness and personal concern of all employees.
5) Raise the quality awareness and personal concerns of all employees.
6) Take actions to correct problems identified through previous steps.
7) Establish a committee for the zero defects program.
8) Train supervisors to actively carry out their part of the quality improvement program.
9) Hold a "zero defects day" to let all employees realize that there has been a change.
10) Encourage individuals to establish improvement goals for themselves and their groups.
11) Encourage employees to communicate to leadership the obstacles they face in attaining their improvement goals.
12) Recognize and appreciate those who participates.

13) Establish quality councils to community on a regular basis.

14) Do it all over again to emphasize that quality improvement never ends.

2:03-TOTAL QUALITY MANAGEMENT CULTURE

The transformation from traditional approaches to Total Quality Management begins with the acceptance of new paradigms. Not only do we improve but also we learn to prosper and thrive in an ever-changing environment. It is helpful to compare the differences between organizations that use traditional methods to those that have implemented Total Quality Management. Areas affected include organizational structure, communication, decision-making regarding products and services, quality, attitudes toward change and improvement and staff development.

In traditional organizations, administrators supervise departments and interactions are through dominantly vertical lines of authority. The managers and specialist staff establish the management environment. Within the system, individual's achievements are rewarded, often fostering competition and resentment among peers. With Total Quality Management, teams direct the work processes, and the management environment grows out of the team structures. All team members have ownership in success, and team-oriented behavior and innovations are valued and recognized. Interactions occur within the teams and through the team processes, not only within departments. Traditionally, decisions are often based on assumptions and gut-level feelings rather that collected data. These decisions are make at the top levels within departments by individual managers and specialists, who dictate improvements to products and services. Departments are isolated in product and service design. Also, the traditional organization decides what to offer customers based on assumptions about customer's needs and preferences and cost of providing or improving products and services often rise according to the availability of funds.

When Total Quality Management is implemented, the commitment to quality ensures that when more resources are available, more is done. The goal is always to offer products and services at a lower cost, focusing on customer satisfaction. The input of identified customers is sought to determine what they want in terms of products and service. Rather than single departments, cross-functional teams develop these products and services, with improvement plans determined by teams of managers, employees, vendors, customers and partner organization. Decisions regarding products and services are based on scientific approaches in Total Quality Management environment. Employees are encouraged to use their intuition to lead them to problems, but trained to verify the nature of problems with hard data. Prevention of problems is the major emphasis with TQM. All work must contribute to the value of the product or service. Work processes that result in waste and errors are not tolerated. Under traditional management, there are standard levels of tolerance for errors and waste. Problems are addressed through inspection and fixing them after they occur. Short-term planning, based primarily on budge cycles, predominates in tradition organizations. The status quo is favored, and work is done according to precedence and pr-existing routines.

By contrast, with Total Quality Management, long-term planning is prevalent and is linked to a continuous focus on the mission of the organization. Change and continuing improvement are desired; innovation and creativity are encouraged; prudent risk is rewarded. This commitment in continuing improvement is reflected in the attitude that training and education of employees represents a valuable investment of resources, and the organization seeks to develop internal quality experts. This differs from the traditional approach, where expertise on quality is sought on the outside and investments in training and education of staff are seen as undesirable and non-productive expenses. The necessary element of commitment is fostered by demonstrations of leadership and cultivation of those who can champion the ideas. The leaders ship the environment by establishing support systems, removing barriers to communication and processes, and reassessing reward and recognition systems. Resources are provided through training, through making time available and through empowerment of individuals.

Envisioning the mission before doing anything else is essential. The vision provides clarity and purpose. Part of the process of developing Total Quality Management is building awareness of the importance of having vision.

To build awareness, leaders often must provide training, using external consultants and demonstrate commitment by their actions. Then, roles, which are in alignment with the mission, evolve based on the consistency of purpose, long-term commitment and customer focus. The entire quality structure grows out of this.

Empowerment means giving authority and responsibility commensurate with skills and maturity to everyone. These empowered individuals can then focus on achieving the vision and focusing involves establishing customer-centered goals based on the mission. The goals must be realistic and have broad applicability. They must be communicated throughout the organization and be relevant to every individual. The goals must then be translated into practice, aligning improvement efforts to organizational objectives. Customers and suppliers, as well as employees, need to share the focus; they need to understand needs, communicate requirements and share experience. At this point, continually improving quality then becomes possible. The organization is able to define standards through the processes of documenting the current status, maintaining and updating existing standards, and measuring performance against these standards. Performance can be evaluated in terms of goals and customer needs.

2:04- PRINCIPLES OF TOTAL QUALITY MANAGEMENT

Total Quality Management has certain underlying principles guiding its efficient and effective implementation.

In a TQM environment, employees use special techniques to capture the voice of the customer, identify and eliminate the root cause of problems, and control unwanted process variation. It integrates the customer information system, complaint handling system, suggestion system, and objective setting system. The new global leaders will be people who can transmit knowledge and power to each member of an organization. This is a total paradigm shift and Total Quality Management responds to this. Successful Total Quality Management requires both behavioral and cultural changes. The organizational management system, human resource management system and the total quality management system must be aligned in a successful TQM initiative. In general, the Total Quality Management environment is built around a specific set of principles, tools, techniques and systems.

The basic principles of Total Quality Management are:

1) Quality can and must be managed
2) Everyone has a customer and is a supplier
3) Processes, not people are the problem
4) Every employee is responsible for quality
5) Problems must be prevented, not just fixed
6) Quality must be measured
7) Quality improvement must be continuous
8) The quality standard is defect-free
9) Goals are based on requirements, not negotiations
10) Life cycle costs, not front end costs
11) Management must be involved and lead
12) Plan and organize for quality improvement

The 21st century workplace will be totally different from what we have now, and its members must be aligned with and own strategic direction of the business, have trust-based work relationships, and be able to build value with one another and their customers. This is the concept of Total Quality Management, or TQM. Leadership in the TQM workplace has to be seen not as a job, based on power and authority, but as a function based on principles, new people skills, and the ability to engage others in coming to consensus around critical decisions and problem solving. This resulting trust and productivity will provide the enterprise a clear competitive advantage.

2:05-TOTAL QUALITY MANAGEMENT AS A FOUNDATION

TQM is the foundation for productive activities in business which include:

1) Meeting Customer Requirements
2) Reducing Development Cycle Times
3) Just in Time/Demand Flow Manufacturing
4) Improvement Teams
5) Reducing Product and Service Costs
6) Improving Administrative System Training

2:06- TEN STEPS TO TOTAL QUALITY MANAGEMENT

Effective and efficient implementation of a TQM strategy requires a systematic procedure involving the following steps:
1) Pursue New Strategic Thinking
2) Know Your Customers
3) Set True Customer Requirements
4) Concentrate on Prevention, not Correction
5) Reduce Chronic Wastes
6) Pursue a Continuous Improvement Strategy
7) Use Structured Methodology for Process Improvement
8) Reduce Variation
9) Use a Balanced Approach
10) Apply to All Functions

Chapter Three

3:00- TOTAL QUALITY MANAGEMENT
PROCESS IMPROVEMENT

The quality improvement process involves planning, organizing and monitoring. This process can, of course, be represented by a flowchart. The way it looks and is done may vary depending on organizational procedures and resources. The objective is the same: to identify problems in processes, thereby preventing compromises in quality in the products or services delivered to customers. It is easier to continue to do things as they always have been done than to scrutinize processes. This is true even when we know there are wasteful, annoying or problematic steps in a process. Processes must be managed and improved. This involves:

1) Defining the process,
2) Measuring process performance (metrics),
3) Reviewing process performance,
4) Identifying process shortcomings,
5) Analyzing process problems,
6) Making a process change,
7) Measuring the effects of the process change,
8) Communicating between employees, supervisors and management.

Total Quality Management offers a process for looking at and improving processes. TQM not only challenges us to change, but provides the tools to facilitate it. These tools focus attention on the way we do things rather than what we accomplish. One tool or technique is to ask the six questions all journalism students are taught to use:

- Who?
- What?
- Where?
- When?
- Why?
- How?

Throughout the steps of planning, organizing and monitoring processes to achieve improvement, these questions are essential. A scientific approach to quality issues is central to TQM. Identification of needs and evaluation of the impact of implemented changes are database. Only the measurement of improvements can prove the effectiveness of changes. Just as quality improvement uses a process-oriented model, problem solving is most easily conceptualized and realized as a process. However, while quality improvements involves focusing on an entire process, problem solving is related to a single area where things are 'stuck." Identification and resolution of the problem is necessary before things can continue. This is often achieved through Process Flow Analysis using Process Flow Charts. In this process, various activities in a project or program are identified and analyzed and evaluated for the most cost-effective, efficient and qualitative method of operation. There are then arranged in a sequence according to how they have to be implemented. This is often in a configuration management format on a floe chart.

Traditionally, management responds to issues, conflicts and defects by reacting to information which is provided (without gathering additional data), assuming causes and fixing the problem. Problem-solving with TQM entails clear steps including recognition, identification and evaluation of possible causes and solutions, selection of a solution to address a specific cause, implementation and monitoring-all accomplished through use of scientific approaches and statistical tools. While these steps may occur in an orderly sequence, the process allows for returning to steps to gain clarification and directions.

3:01- PROCESS FLOW CHART

A flow chart is a pictorial representation describing a process being studied or used to plan the stages of a project. It provides people with a common language or reference point when dealing with a project or process. Flow charts provide an excellent form of documentation for a process and are useful when examining how various steps in a process work together. The American National Standards Institute (ANSI) established its own symbols, which are used to analyze the second condition of a flow chart process.

Flowcharting is a graphic representation of a series of steps that are performed in a specific work process. The important uses of Flowcharting are:

1) Identifying the actual path that a product or service follows to show redundancies, inefficiencies and misunderstandings,
2) Creating a common understanding of the work process,
3) Identifying customers previously neglected,
4) Identifying opportunities for improvement,
5) Identifying the ideal path for a product or service,
6) Setting boundaries.

General Process Activities Sequence

Generally, process development and management has a sequence for information input, processing and generating results or output. The process flow can be represented as follows:

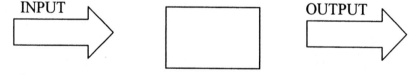

Chart 3:01.

A flowchart contains symbols to identify activities or sequential steps beginning, end and decision points; connections or relationships; and the direction or path, which is followed in the process.

Flowchart symbols help to describe various activities in process development. The Processing or Activity symbol is a description of the activity it represents. The Decision symbol represents a point in the process where a decision or question arises. From there, the process branches into two or more paths depending on the answer that appears. The terminal symbol identifies the beginning or end of a process. The Connector shows a viewer that the diagram continues on another page. Overall, the flowchart helps in the analysis and evaluation of activities to identify inefficiencies, unnecessary loops, process breakdown and opportunities for simplification and improvement.

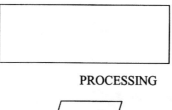

PROCESSING

INPUT/OUTPUT

DECISION

TERMINAL

CONNECTOR

Chart: 3:02. Process Flow Chart Symbols

3:02- TOTAL QUALITY MANAGEMENT TOOLS

These are statistical methods for analyzing numerical data and focusing on results.

3:02:01-Affinity Diagrams

Hierarchical groups of language data with similar thoughts and ideas are sorted together in columns and groups. The purpose is to find missing information such as problems, causes, ideas, solutions and customer requirements.

3:02:02- Tree Diagrams

This is used to find missing categories of information in a structure, usually an organizational chart. This should be top-to-bottom vice versa.

3:02:03- Matrix Diagrams

This defines the levels of relationships between two groups of factors. It helps to visualize and simplify the complex relationships between two groups of factors.

3:02:04- Gantt Charts

This represents a graphical schedule for each task, action or activity necessary to achieve a target or purpose.

3:02:05- Relationship Diagrams

It shows the degree of drive or influence of a cause on an effect. This determines the cause and effect relationships between many issues so as to visualize logical patterns within them.

3:02:06- Process Decision Charts

It outlines problems and barriers to a predetermined outcome and the corrective actions to be taken if the problems and barriers occur.

3:02:07- Cause and Effects Charts

This can sometimes be displayed using a fishbone and this organizes factors and variables that potentially impact quality, causes of problems and obstacles to the achievement of goals

3:03- TOTAL QUALITY MANAGEMENT STATISTICAL TOOLS

Total Quality Management relies on data collection and analysis for objective decision-making. The graphic display of data through statistical tools such as charts and graphs makes it easy to see and understand current status, variations, relative importance of factors, and effectiveness of changes compared to desired impact.

Although there are a wide variety of statistical tools available, including the flowchart, the following six are used most frequently within the quality improvement process: Pareto chart, run chart, control chart, scatter diagram, histogram, and the pie chart. A basic understanding of how to develop and use these tools is needed to implement TQM.

3:03:01- Data Sheets

This is data entry in a table of rows and columns or on single cards. It helps to organize, manage and track data and to calculate relationships between data.

125	0.2	15	21	5	15
130	0.3	20	26	10	20
135	0.5	25	31	15	25
140	0.6	30	36	20	30
145	0.8	40	41	25	35
150	0.7	45	46	30	40

3:03:02- Pareto Charts

This derives its name from the Pareto Principle, which states that 805 of the effects come from 20% of the causes. The chart is a series of vertical bars with their heights reflecting the frequency, cost or impact of the problems.

The data points drawn as proportionally sized bars and ranked by size, with or without a line indicating cumulative total with the addition of each item.

3:03:03- Bar Charts

This represents data points drawn as proportionally sized, side-by-side or stacked bars. It helps to compare distinct non-continuous items.

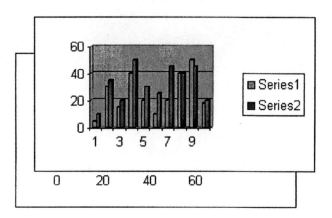

3:03:04- Run Charts

Run charts are also known as trend charts and used to measure change over time. It shows trends, cycles and deviations and illustrates good and bad situations in a process.

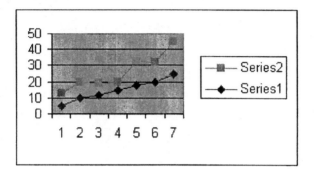

3:03:05- Pie Charts

These are graphical display of relative magnitudes or frequencies of data categories. They help to visualize the proportions and relative importance of contributing items and clearly show frequencies, place, or other data classification, which represents the largest share.

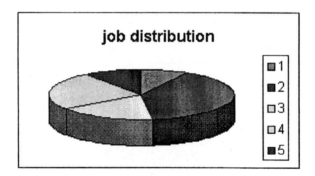

3:03:06- Histograms

This is also called a bar chart or graph and displays variation or distribution of measured data it compares distribution, determines means and modes, and identifies population control limits, mixtures, abnormality or errors.

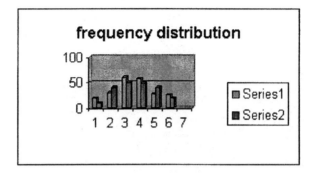

3:03:07- Scatter Diagrams

These are also known as scatter gram or correlation charts and show the relationship between variables. It helps to analyze the correlation between two variables. And to predict future relationships based upon past correlations.

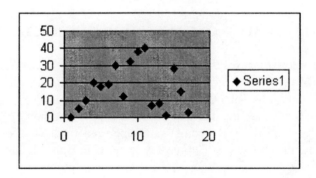

3:03:08- Control Charts

A control chart is used to track important conditions over time and also to indicate the range of variation in a system or process. They are used for continuous values such as length, weight or concentration. Control charts determine whether process characteristics consistently approach extreme control limits. They also determine whether a process is in or out of control.

Chapter Four

4:00- TOTAL QUALITY MANAGEMENT ORGANIZATION

4:01- QUALITY ORGANIZATIONAL STRUCTURE

The essential element for a successful quality program is the development of an organizational structure that will institute, sustain and facilitate the expansion of the Total Quality Management process. The quality structure consists of three distinct elements, (the Quality Council, Panels and the Quality Improvement Teams), all supported by a Quality Planning and Development Division. But the key factor here is the alignment among various organizational systems such as human resource systems, including job design, selection processes, compensation and rewards, performance appraisal, training and development that must align and support the new TQM culture. Another system consideration is that TQM should evolve from the strategic plan and be based on stakeholder expectations.

4:01:01- The Executive Council- its main functions are: -

• Creating the strategic vision
• Developing the philosophy
• Promoting and championing the vision
• Establishing the TQM culture

4:01:02- The Quality Council

The Quality Council consists of a leader (i.e. the Executive Director) and the senior functional managers. The major responsibilities of the Quality Council are:

- Developing and implementing policy.
- Developing and implementing the TQM organizational plan.
- Creating and sustaining TQM teams.
- Overseeing regulations and financial responsibilities.
- Recommending training.
- Facilitating communication.
- Removing barriers that inhibit progress with quality improvements.
- Ensuring the organization's vision is promoted and implemented.

4:01:03- TQM Panels

The functions of Panels in a Total Quality Management implementation process can be summarized as follows:

- Identifying process improvement areas.
- Reviewing process improvements.
- Consulting with TQM teams.
- Coordinating with the Division of Quality Planning and Development.
- Reviewing requests for process improvement opportunities.
- Setting thresholds for evaluations.
- Reviewing performance against thresholds.
- Determining on-going M & E's based team recommendations.

4:01:04:- Quality Management Teams

Teams are the focus of activity in Total Quality Management. The success of a team depends on the clarity of its mission, defined decision-making process, openly established and accepted ground rules, education in problem-solving methods, contribution of its members, optimism about outcome and the supportive nature of members to the teams goals and dedication for its success, cooperative relationship, constructive behaviors, enthusiasm, congruity, common purpose, progressiveness and openness.

The two main types of Quality Improvement Teams are Cross-Functional and Department Teams.

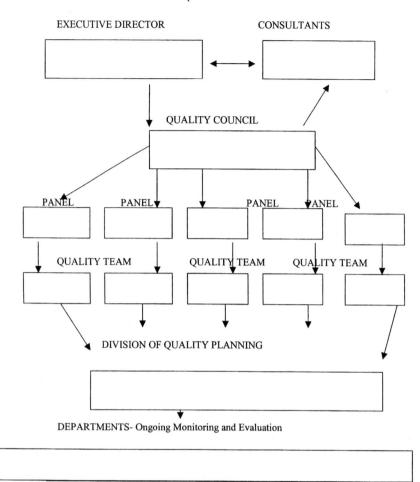

EXECUTIVE DIRECTOR   CONSULTANTS

QUALITY COUNCIL

PANEL   PANEL   PANEL   ANEL

QUALITY TEAM   QUALITY TEAM   QUALITY TEAM

DIVISION OF QUALITY PLANNING

DEPARTMENTS- Ongoing Monitoring and Evaluation

Chart4:01.   Quality Organizational Structure

4:01:04:01-Cross-Functional Teams

Cross-functional Teams are and exciting and innovative way of solving problems and dealing with issues that affect large portions of an organization. Cross-functional quality improvement team members are selected from several work units, since the problem they will be given affects many areas of the organization, not just one department. Each cross-functional team consists of 6–8 members who work on a specific problem to completion in approximately 3–6 months. These teams, through the application of the principles and tools of TQM, will analyze the given process, collect data, recommend process improvements, implement the improvements and report the findings.

4:01:04:02- Departmental Teams

A Department Process Improvement Team follows the same procedure as a Cross-Functional Team when solving an identified problem, but with one major difference: Departmental Teams are concerned with department issues. These teams, regardless of how you chose to label them, need to be differentiated from the Cross-Functional and Departmental Quality Improvement Teams. Self-managed teams can have as many as 30 members, are on-going, work in or on a specific job or task, are accountable for the entire team's work and manage themselves to the extent designated by their supervisors.

Although there may be times when a self-managed team uses the more structured process of a TQM team, most of their efforts are directed toward day-to-day decisions involving projects and changes within their specific unit. In other words, they will rarely need to use the more involved procedures outlined in this handbook.

Regardless of your type of team, it is important to learn and practice good team building skills, and it is also important to keep accurate records and to fulfill your other administrative responsibilities so that your team's success (and difficulties) can be used to help your entire organization. After all, the purpose of quality teams is to find ways to make the organization more effective so that, in turn, everyone from customers to employees to stockholders reaps the benefits.

4:02-TEAM ROLES AND RESPONSIBILITIES

TQM Process Teams are composed of a Team Leader, Team Facilitator and Team Members. TQM teams generally have 6–8 members who have been given one specific process to improve. Teams generally meet weekly and complete their task within a 3–6 month period.

4:02: 01- Team Leader

The role of the Team Leader is to guide the team through the process improvement structure to achieve a successful outcome. The Team Leader conducts the meeting, coordinates arrangements, instructs team members in the process, ensures proper documentation and interfaces with Quality Council, consultants, etc. In other words, the team leader provides direction and focus on the team's activities.

4:02: 02- Team Facilitator

The role of the Team Facilitator is to promote effective group dynamics so the team can achieve its goal. The team facilitator's specific responsibilities consist of synthesizing ideas, mediating and resolving conflicts, getting honest responses from all members, assisting with training and providing feedback to the team. The facilitator must be a person who does not have a vested interest (or responsibility) in the process being improved. He or she must also be capable of remaining objective with each member. The facilitator must be skilled in the quality tools, techniques and structure, as well as group processes. For Further information regarding this important role, see Section III of this handbook.

4:02:03- Team Recorder

The recorder's role is to capture the basic ideas of the group, usually writing on boards in full view of members. He remains neutral and unbiased.

4:02:04- Team Members

The role of Team Members is to share knowledge and expertise by participating fully in the improvement process. Major responsibilities include participating in all meetings, recognizing that serving on a team is part of one's "real job", adhering to the team's ground rules, performing outside team assignments, serving as timekeeper or recorder, as requested, and implementing recommendations. Team Members are an integral part in the organizational quality implementation program. Therefore, commitment is a key work for all team members. Without responsibility and committed team members, the team's goal (and the organization's goal) will not be achieved.

4:03:- TRADITIONAL MANAGEMENT AND INTEGRATED MANAGEMENT (TQM) COMPARED

4:03:01-Traditional Management:

In this approach TQM never becomes an accepted reality by either organization or human resource management. It is usually seen as a competing force or "something to be tolerated". This approach represents 80% failure of TQM implementation. The TQM system consumes valuable resources needed by the other systems and rejection begins to occur. Some of the characteristics of traditional management are:

1. Authoritative Management—the Director takes decision without consulting any lower authorities.
2. Competition is discouraged—career enhance is not emphasized to avoid other people climbing the corporate ladder.

3. Communication flows in one direction—from the top to the bottom—with an authoritative management style information is disseminated generally from the director to lower authorities and not vice versa
4. Product and service design are dictated by managers—most workers are like "assembly line" workers who are just there to implement decisions. There is no opportunity for suggestions or change in workflow dictated by the higher authority.
5. Decisions are based on assumptions—the management does not often analyze and evaluate situations before taking decisions. It is always assumed that everything will be accomplished.
6. Quality assurance is based on inspection and fixing problems—traditional management does not take a preventive approach to certain problems because it is assumed that all projects will materialize.
7. Status-quo is preferred; precedence prevails—most managers in traditional management do not want changes in the administration and so prefer people to stay in positions indefinitely even if they are not productive.
8. Training is non-productive—since changes and career enhancement is not encouraged sometimes they see no need for any form of training in the organization so employees are often are often not very conversant with contemporary issues affecting organizations as well employees benefits.

Most traditional management organizational structures are functional and communication and decision-making is mostly vertical-from top to bottom.

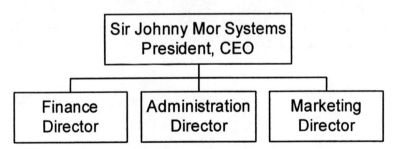

Chart 4:02. Typical Traditional Management Organizational Structure

4:03:02- Integrated Management (TQM)

In this approach, a Total Quality Management concept is blended and balanced with existing cultural initiatives in both organizational and human resource management systems. This approach represents 20% success of most of TQM implementation. Some of the characteristics of the management approach are:

1. Empowered teams direct processes—decisions emanate from panels and teams which are often "cross-functional" and made up of employees from various departments in the organization.
2. Trust and collaboration are developed—working in panels and teams makes employees to understand each other better. This helps to create a very trusting relationship among employees.
3. Communication flows up, down and horizontal—information flows in all directions in the organization since everyone is involved in decision-making.
4. Teams and Panels perform product and service designs—they deliberate on the strategic development and implementation of company goals and objectives.
5. Decisions are based on facts and scientific approaches—there is often a lot of analysis and evaluation of facts and figures before decisions are made.
6. Quality improvement is based on problem prevention—there is very meticulous planning with provision for maintenance and contingency to avoid irreparable problems
7. Innovation, creativity and risk-taking are encouraged—employees are empowered to be original in thought, ingenuous and inventive towards the development of services or products in the organization.
8. Investment in training is extremely valuable—there is often a lot of provision for in-service and professional training for clients to acquire the necessary skills and knowledge in order to remain competitive in the market place. Sometimes employees are offered scholarships to universities for professional studies which are of benefit to the organization. Tuition reimbursement also helps employees to complete such professional and academic studies while working.

4:04:- TOTAL QUALITY MANAGEMENT AND THE PARADIGM SHIFT

Paradigms are a way that we perceive and understand the world and understanding the power of paradigms is vital to personal effectiveness and growth. The paradigms we embody can be enlightening, allowing us to experience new and wonderful things, but can just be as blinders that shield us from new thoughts or experiences. We need to change and update what is around us- make paradigm shifts. The power of shifting paradigms is all around us, but so is the failure that results when we are resistant to change. So is the TQM process. Recognizing and understanding the power of our personal paradigms and those of our organizations is very important for us to adjust to organizational changes. Personal computers, fax machines, cellular phones, automated banking machines, solar-powered calculators, laser printers, anti-lock automobile brakes, compact discs and digital video disc (DVD) players are all items that would be unthinkable a few years ago. This been a great paradigm shift in the lives of individual and organizations.

4:05:- TQM AND THE INTERNATIONAL ORGANIZATION FOR STANDARDIZATION (ISO) SERIES STANDARDS

The International Organization for Standardization (ISO) standardizes, organizes and controls operations in the manufacturing and service industries. It provides for consistent dissemination of information, improves various aspects of the business-based use of statistical data and analysis, acceptance of the system as a standard for ensuring quality in a global market, enhancing customer responsiveness to products and services and encouraging improvement. The standards are useful to industrial and business organizations of all types, to governmental and other regulatory bodies, to trade officials, to conformity assessment officials, to suppliers and customers of products and services in public and private sectors, and to people in general as consumers and end users.

The ISO Quality Standard sets in place a system to depend on a strategy whose implementation is the basis for a Total Quality Management system. The standards contribute to making the development, manufacturing and supply of products and services more efficient, safer and cleaner and trade between countries easier and fairer, which is the fundamental philosophy of the Total Quality Management concept. They provide the basis for health, safety and environmental legislation as well as technology transfer.

The ISO 8000-2000 family of Standards was developed to assist organizations and sizes, to implement and operate an effective and efficient quality management system made of four core standards: -

- 9001 Model—this is for quality assurance in design, development, production, installation and servicing,
- 9002 Model—this is uses for quality assurance in production, installation and servicing,
- 9003 Model—this is implemented for quality assurance in final inspection and test,
- 9004 Model—this represents guidelines for development of quality system elements and management.

The ISO 9000 series provides the company with a quality system that: -
1) Standardizes, organizes and controls operations,
2) Provides for consistent dissemination of information,
3) Improves various aspects of the business—based use of statistical data and analysis,
4) Acceptance of the system as a standard for ensuring quality in a global market,
5) Enhances customer responsiveness to products and service,
6) Encourages improvement.

The ISO 9000 series standards are organized according to functions, such as: document and data control, and contract review therefore they are set forth in a logical format. Organized in outline form they provide a template for each function that affects the quality of the product or service in the company. Guidelines provided by the standards establish a consistent approach to policy documentation. Controls are set forth in the standards in the areas of document control of non-conforming product. Three areas of the standards, in particular, provide for consistent dissemination of information for the following control elements:

• Control of quality—Records insures that pertinent records are maintained regarding quality records.
• Design control—this process eliminates ad-hoc engineering changes that are not communicated with all parties involved in the process.
• Document and data control—this process helps in document revision, document distribution, removal of obsolete documents, and document approval.

The ISO 9000 series standards require the company to identify the need for statistical techniques and to implement and control such techniques. The standards specifically point to process capability and product characteristics. The standards allow the company the flexibility to use those statistical techniques that would be appropriate for their industry. Additionally, the standards refer to the use of both corrective and preventative action, and effective internal auditing. These techniques and systems improve business processes by using database management rather than instinct and hunches.

The World Standardization Day is being celebrated around the world and in 2004; it was celebrated in the Republic of Cameroon under the theme, "Standardization Connects the World". This helps to protect the security of consumers, the economy, local industries, the environment and guarantees company loyalty, ameliorate productivity and competition, and promote investment and growth. Cameroon has instituted the "National Quality Week" five years ago in order to educate and inform businesses to operate in conformity with the standards set by the International Organization for Standardization (ISO).

Chapter Five

5:00- THE STATE OF AFRICAN HEALTH AND HUMAN RESOURCES: PROBLEMS AND POTENTIALS

5:01-THE STATE OF HEALTH IN AFRICA

Widespread disease and poverty continue to plague millions of people in Africa. The AIDS epidemic has had a disproportionate toll on the continent, as 25.3 million of the 36.1 million people living with HIV/AIDS are found in sub-Saharan Africa. More than 13 million cases of measles occur and 450,000 children die from the disease in Africa each year. In addition, malaria, acute respiratory infections, and diarrhea are among the leading causes of death for children under five years of age.

The gravity of health problem is compounded because many African countries lack the resources and infrastructure to manage the economic and health systems of many diseases. Without continued international support and effective health services to help Africans cope with these deadly diseases, African society will continue to suffer unnecessary preventable tragedies. The vast majority of these tragedies can be migrated and even eradicated with simple, effective preventative measures.

The United Nations approach to Africa's health crisis is through the following strategies:

1) Holistic Approach:

Improving the health and well being of children and adolescents in Africa requires a holistic and coordinated approach. The United Nations Foundation (UN Foundation) promotes both community-based preventive health measures and adolescent empowerment to ensure improved health status and sustainable development. The UN Foundation plans to continue to focus on strategic heath initiatives that foster healthy children, adolescents, and women—their families and communities.

2) *Preventive Health for Children:*

(Integrated management of Childhood Illnesses (IMCI)
  IMCI, a World Health Organization/United Nations Children's Fund Initiative seeks to improve growth and development among children less than five years of age. IMCI's integrated approach aims to prevent child death and illness in three ways such as improving family and community health practices; strengthening the skills of health staff; enhancing the health delivery system. The UN Foundation has supported community IMCI in countries such as Madagascar, Malawi, and Tanzania. The community IMCI program has demonstrated early positive impact on the lives of children and their families.

3) *Strengthening Immunization Services in Africa:*

The Measles Initiative is a long-term commitment to control the 450,000 annual measles death in Africa by supporting immunization services, including vaccinating 200 million children through both mass and follow-up campaigns in up to 36 sub-Saharan African countries. The UN Foundation is one of five partners who together are committing $200 million over five years in order to end measles deaths in Africa by 2005.

4) *Adolescent Girls: Empowering and Educating-*

While protecting African children from deadly diseases is imperative, protecting these health investments is equally important in the second decade of life. Adolescents face particular vulnerabilities, combined with limited educational and economic opportunities, in their transition to adulthood. It is during these years that risks of early or unintended pregnancy, HIV infection, and forced or early marriage, pose detrimental and often life-threatening consequences to their health and future.

5) *Southern Africa Youth Initiative:*

The Southern Africa Youth Initiative is an example of a coordinated multi-country, multi-agency United Nations (UN) response that focuses on arming adolescent girls with the resources to fight infection. Multisectoral interventions include improved health care services, community support, peer education, micro-credit, health insurance, and livelihood training. Partnering with such organizations as the Joint UN Program on HIV/AIDS (UNAIDS), United Nations Population Fund (UNFPA), United Nations Children's Fund (UNICEF), United Nations Development Program (UNDP), and International Labor Organization (ILO), the UN Foundation is ensuring that adolescent girls get the resources they need to survive and thrive.

6) The UN Foundation and the Global Fund:

In order to combat some of the most life-threatening diseases that are devastating sub-Saharan Africa, the UN established the Global Fund to Fight AIDS, Tuberculosis, and Malaria. The Global Fund provides grants to public, private and non-governmental programs that support the prevention, treatment, care, and support of the infected and potentially infected. The UN Foundation has established a special account to receive contributions from individuals, corporations, and organizations wishing to support the fight against AIDS, tuberculosis and malaria.

Table 5:01. Some Mortality statistics by various categories of diseases from the World Health Report 2002 can be represented as follows:

	WORLD			AFRICA
	Both Sexes	Males	Females	Child/Adult
Population (000)	6,122,210	33,083,884	3,038,327	353,598
TOTAL DEATHS	56,554	29,628	26,926	6,316
1) Communicable Diseases	18,374	9,529	8,846	4,615
a) Infectious and Parasitic	10,937	5,875	5,062	3,525
b) Respiratory Infections	3,947	2.053	1,894	584
c) Maternal Conditions	509	0	509	143
d) Nutritional Deficiencies	477	219	264	80
2) Non-Communicable Diseases	33,077	16,726	16,352	1,264
a) Malignant Neoplasms	7,115	3,952	3,163	303
b) Diabetes Millitus	895	401	495	35
c) Neuropsychiatric Dis.	1.023	529	506	44
d) Cardiovascular Diseases	16,585	7,062	8,623	503
e) Respiratory Diseases	3,560	1,181	1,742	129
f) Digestive Diseases	1,987	1,108	879	108
g) Genitourinary Diseases	825	450	375	64
h) Skin Diseases	67	29	38	12
i) Musculoskeletal Diseases	119	38	74 7	
j) Congenital Abnormalities	507	257	249	38
k) Oral Diseases	2	1	1	0
l) Injuries	5,103	3,374	1,729	437
m) Accidents	3,508	2,251	1,257	251

Source: The World Health Report-2002

Table 5:02, **Some Regional Health Indicators in Africa**

Indicator	Sub-Saharan Africa	North Africa/ Middle East
Total Population	688.4 million	305.8 million
Population Growth (annual %)	2.3	1.9
Life Expectancy (years)	45.8	68.6
Fertility Rate (birth per woman)	5.1	3.1
Infant Mortality Rate (per 1,000 live birth)	103.1	43.7
Under 5 mortality rate (per 1,000 children)	173.9	54.1
Child Immunization, measles (% of under 12 months)	57.6	92.0
Prevalence of HIV (female, % ages 15–24)	57.6	Not indicated
Literacy total (% of ages 15 and above)	64.9	67.2
Literacy female (% of ages 15 and above)	57.5	60.9
Primary school completion rate (% of age group)	57.5	82.9
Net secondary enrollment (% of age group)	Not indicated	54.4

Source: World Health Report, 2002

7) *The United Nations Foundation:*

The United Nations Foundation (UN Foundation) was created in 1998 with businessman and philanthropist R.E. Turner's historic gift to support United Nations (UN) causes. The United Nation Foundation's mission is to support the goals and objectives of the UN and its Charter, in order to promote a more peaceful, prosperous, and just world—with special emphasis on the United Nations work on behalf of economic, social, environmental, and humanitarian causes.

5:02- THE HEALTHCARE CRISIS IN AFRICA

In 1948, African and G8 member states were amongst the General Assembly of UN countries that adopted the Universal Declaration on Human Rights. Article 25 of the Declaration proclaims:

> "Everyone has the right to a standard of living adequate for the health and well-being of himself and his family, including food, clothing, housing and medical care and necessary social services, and the right to security in the

event of unemployment, sickness, disability, widowhood, old age or other lack of livelihood in circumstances beyond this control".

Just over 50 years later, in a global survey commissioned for the Millennium Summit of the United Nations by UN Secretary Kofi Annan, good health consistently ranked as the number one desire. This view is supported by economic analysis and the recent Report of the Commission on Macroeconomics and Health confirmed that health is a priority goal in its own right, as well as a central input into economic development and poverty reduction. The importance of investing in health has been greatly underestimated, not only by analysis but also by developing-country governments and the international donor community.

The New Partnerships for African Development (NEPAD) report of October 2001 states that health is one of the critical challenges to narrowing the gap between Africa and high-income nations. G8 member states share a responsibility for helping to find solutions to this development gap and to the negative impacts of globalization on health. In a globalize world, the economic development and stability of all countries is inter-dependent. There-

Table 5:03. Some Country Specific Healthcare Indicators (2001)

Indicator	Country				
	Zimbabwe	Kenya	Nigeria	Senegal	South Africa
Life Expectancy at birth, total (years)	39.5	46.3	46.1	52.3	47.1
Mortality rate, infant (per 1,000 live birth)	76.0	78.0	110.0	79.0	56.0
Fertility rate, total (births per woman)	3.7	4.3	4.6	5.0	2.8
Population growth (annual %)	1.1	1.9	22	24	28
Illiteracy rate, adult total (% of people 16 and above)	10.7	16.7	34.6	61.7	14.4
Health Expenditure per couple (current US $)	16	24	21	23	256
Immunization, DPT (% of children under 12 months)	75.0	76.0	26.0	52.0	81.0
Immunization Measles (% of children under 12 months)	68.0	76.0	40.0	48.0	72.0
Improved water source (% of population with access)	85.0	49.0	57.0	78.0	88.0
Prevalence of HIV (% of population 15–40)	33.7	13.9	5.1	1.6	19.9

Source: World Health Organization (2001)

fore, global prosperity depends on our ability to improve the health of all the world's people, including those in the poorest countries of Africa.

While there have been substantial improvements in health in Africa in the last several decades, this progress has been uneven and incomplete. Of even greater concern is the fact that, in several countries, the gains of the past are being reversed. Instead of improvement, we are witnessing the deterioration of several health indicators such as infant mortality, particularly in sub-Saharan Africa. Compared with other regions in the world, Africa has the lowest life expectancy, highest infant mortality rates, and largest projected population growth:

* Life expectancy is 54 years (life expectancy in Canada is 79 years),
* The infant mortality rate is 88.0 per 1000 live births,
* The birth rate is 38-births/year/1000 total populations
* Immunization rates have declined from 62% in 1990 to 47% in 1999,

Sub-Saharan Africa accounts for 90% of the world's 300–500 million clinical cases of malaria per year. Of the estimated over 1 million deaths each year worldwide, the vast majority occur among young children and pregnant women in Africa, especially in remote rural areas with poor access to health services. This strategy is again being used to restore this country's health system, supported by an investment in health spending of 12% of the government budget. The Tanzania Health Intervention Project (TEHIP) illustrates the importance of knowledge-based planning by Council Health Management Teams (CHMTs) in a decentralized health system. The project has demonstrated that CHMT's can use evidence to set priorities, allocate resources and monitor health impacts.

In Africa now, several problem and discipline specific health research networks have been established at regional levels and some good examples are:

1) Equinet (Network on Equity in Health in Southern Africa):

This is a network of research, civil society 15 and health sector organizations. Equinet's main aim is to build alliances leading to positive policies on health at both local and regional levels.

2) Multilateral Initiative for Malaria (MIM):

This is an alliance of organizations and individuals concerned with malaria. It aims to maximize the impact of scientific research against malaria in Africa, through promoting capacity building and facilitating global collaboration and coordination.

3) Social Sciences and Medicine Africa Network (SOMA-Net):

The goal of this organization is to develop health social science research capacity and promote development oriented research that informs and strengthens health development and contributes to global knowledge.

4) International Network for the continuous Demographic Evaluation of Populations and Their Health (INDEPTH):

This network consists of 29 health and demographic evaluation sites situated in 16 countries, all but 2 of which are in Africa. The goal is to enhance substantially the capabilities of INDEPTH sites through technical strengthening, methodological development, widened applications to policy and practice, and increased interaction of site leaders, researchers, and managers.

5) Global Equity Gauge Alliance (GEGA):

This alliance is dedicated to the promotion of equity in health through effective advocacy and community action based upon reliable monitoring information. Equity Gauges measure aspects of the health care system, but above all are concerned with gaps in health status between population groups. A particular focus is placed on the social determinants of health disparities. Monitoring initiatives have been launched in six African countries.

Several other organizations deserve special mention such as the Global Business Coalition on HIV/AIDS, the Global Health Initiative Task Force of the World Economic Forum, the World Health Organization's Roll Back Malaria initiative and the Corporate Council on Africa. These organizations and others like them are dedicated to mobilizing the resources and skills of private companies in improving public health. Exxon Mobil is actively involved in their work.

The African health research community has put forward some key implementation strategies for advancing health research in Africa. They include the following:

*Strengthen capacity of African institutions through sustained funding for human resources, physical infrastructure, information and communication technologies, and networks.

Per capita expenditure on health has generally been very low and small in most African countries and this has had some very serious negative effects and impact on healthcare service delivery as shown on the table below from the World Health Organization performance review in 2001. The health expenditures also represent a very small percentage of the Gross National Product (GNP) of these countries. This is persistent and remains a dilemma in the African healthcare industry.

Table 5:04.   African Health Expenditures ($) per capita and % of GNP (2001)

No.	County	Per Capita Expenditure on Health	% of GNP
1	South Africa	652	8.3
2	Tunisia	463	6.8
3	Botswana	381	6.6
4	Namibia	342	7.5
5	Libya	239	8.6
6	Morocco	199	5.9
7	Gabon	197	3.9
8	Algeria	169	4.7
9	Swaziland	167	3.6
10	Egypt	153	3.2
11	Zimbabwe	142	6.5
12	Cote d'Ivoire	127	6.6
13	Liberia	127	4.1
14	Kenya	114	7.5
15	Equatorial Guinea	106	2.1
16	Lesotho	101	5.4
17	Djibouti	90	2.3
18	Gambia	78	6.3
19	Angola	70	2.3
20	Senegal	63	4.5
21	Guinea	61	2.3
22	Ghana	60	4.8
23	Central African Republic	58	4.1
24	Uganda	57	5.2
25	Zambia	52	5.7
26	Mozambique	47	5.1
27	Mauritania	45	3.3
28	Togo	45	2.2
29	Rwanda	44	5.2
30	Cameroon	42	3.5
31	Sudan	39	4.3
32	Malawi	39	7.3
33	Benin	39	4.1
34	Guinea-Bissau	37	5.5
35	Eritrea	36	5.3
36	Nigeria	31	3.2
37	Mali	30	4.3
38	Burkina Faso	27	3.3
39	Sierra Leone	26	4.5
40	Tanzania	26	4.4
41	Congo	22	2.2
42	Niger	22	3.1
43	Burundi	19	3.2
44	Chad	17	2.1
45	Ethiopia	14	3.1
46	Dem. Rep of Congo	12	3.3
47	Somalia	10	2.00

Source: WHO World Health Report 2004

5:03- THE AFRICAN HUMAN RESOURCE POTENTIAL AND DILEMMA

Human resources refer to people power made up various individuals and professionals in an organization.

The human resource problem in the health sector in sub-Saharan Africa has reached crisis proportions in many countries and although, the gravity of the problem varies across the region, the situation in some countries is so grave that urgent action is needed. A complex set of factors has contributed to this problem, some exogenous, such as the austere fiscal measures introduced by Structural Adjustment Program (SAP). Production of health workers has not kept pace with need, especially with the ever-increasing burden of disease brought about by the HIV/AIDS and resurgent epidemics. Some countries have focused on producing more expensive cadres of health workers relative to their disease burden and relative to what they can afford to sustain. In addition, the scope of professional practice by each cadre has been too rigid and inflexible, considering the African health settings in which they work. Many government health workers lack motivation because they are poorly paid, poorly equipped, infrequently supervised and informed, and have limited career opportunities within the civil service. Many medical, technical, and managerial positions are now vacant, and scarce medically personnel are often misused for management tasks. Capital from donor organizations devoted to training and human resource development, though large in some countries, have been poorly coordinated and have not addressed the underlying cause of poor staff motivation.

Personnel management systems are highly centralized and weak, and human resource planning and management has not been given the importance it deserves. New structures, practices, and technologies are imposing a heavy strain on an already weak human resource base in the health sector. According to the World Bank and WHO/AFRO on "Building Strategic Partnership in Education in Health in Africa" held in Addis Ababa, Ethiopia from January 29 to February 1, 2002, poor morale may be engendering adoptive and counter-productive behavior among health workers. Some of the recommendations were:

1) Adopting a "systems approach" to diagnose Human Resource problems,
2) Improving the human resource information base and conduct human-resource country case assessments, which can point to the critical gaps that need to be urgently addressed,
3) Reducing the rigid professional practice barriers to enable health workers to take on additional functions, increase and improve service delivery, and reduce costs,

4) Reviewing the relevance of training programs, professionalize the selection of trainees, and experiment with alternative training methods,
5) Adopting where feasible, more flexible employment and provider arrangements, including contracting services and management to private partners,
6) Shifting gradually towards results-oriented performance management,
7) Providing greater authority and better information to local managers for personnel management and employed relations, and
8) Clarifying the definition of staff responsibilities and performance and keep workers informed and inspired.

In general, the health personnel to population ratios in Africa have been high and always lagged behind the rest of the world. In the 1980s, one doctor catered to 10,800 persons in sub-Saharan Africa, compared to 1,400 in all developing countries and 300 in industrial countries. In fact, ten countries have 1 doctor per 30,000 populations and thirty-one countries do not meet World Health Organization's "Health for All" standard of 1 doctor per 5000 population.

Budgetary stringency reduces African governments' ability to attract, retain, and maintain the morale of professional health workers as treasures as unable to upgrade salaries and working conditions, especially of skilled staff. On other hand, because medical and nursing training in Africa is mostly government-provided or financed, fiscal crises have also severely limited governments' capacity to train health workers. This pressure on the production and retention of health workers has created shortages in such key cadres as doctors, clinical officers, medical assistants, nurses, midwives, and laboratory technicians. The

Table 5: 05. African Countries by Population Per Doctor Ratio

	Population Per Doctor	Countries
1	1 per 30.000 or more	Burkina Faso, Central African Republic, Chad, Eritrea, Ethiopia, Gambia, Malawi, Mozambique, Niger and Tanzania
2	1 per 20.000	Angola, Benin, Comoro Island, D.R. of Congo, Lesotho, Mali, Rwanda, Sierra Leone, Somalia, Togo, Uganda, Zambia
3	1 per 10.000	Burundi, Cameroon, Cote d'Ivoire, Djibouti, Ghana, Madagascar, Senegal, Sudan, Swaziland
1	1 per 5.000	Botswana, Cape Verde, Republic of Congo, Gabon, Equatorial Guinea, Guinea, Guinea-Bissau, Kenya, Mauritania, Mauritius, Namibia, Nigeria, Sao Tome and Principe, Seychelles, Swaziland, South Africa, Zimbabwe.

Source: WHO (2002): Estimates of Health Personnel-1998

Table 5:06. African Countries by Population Per Nurse Ratio

	Population Per Nurse	Countries
1	1 per 10.000 or more	Central African Republic, Gambia, Mali
2	1 per 5.000	Benin, Burkina Faso, Chad, Eritrea, Madagascar, Niger, Senegal, Togo, Uganda
3	1 per 2.000	Cape Verde, Comoros Islands, Cote d'Ivoire, DR Congo, Equatorial Guinea, Ghana, Guinea, Lesotho, Sierra Leone, Sudan
4	1 per 1.000	Angola, Botswana, Djibouti, DR Congo, Guinea-Bissau, Kenya, Mauritania, Mauritius, Namibia, Nigeria, Sao Tome and Principe, Seychelles, South Africa, Tanzania, Zambia, Zimbabwe

Source: WHO (2002): Estimates of Health Personnel-1998

total number of health workers in most African countries is actually quite large, but most of the workers are unskilled or lowly trained. The poorly coordinated expansion of the health-facility network in many African countries has also contributed to the human resource problem in a major way. In many countries, the construction and refurbishment of health facilities has outpaced the health system's ability to staff and maintain them on a sustainable basis. In Mali, the government aggressively expanded the number of community health posts to 533, but by January 2001, only 43 percent were found operational, the rest having been closed for lack of personnel.

The movement from the civil service for more lucrative local employment has also marked the African health-sector labor market in recent years. A major factor has been the rather quick liberalization of medical practice in such countries as Malawi, Mozambique, and Tanzania resulting in the movement of trained medical civil servants to private practice, either individually or with nonprofit or for-profit health providers. Health service providers (especially doctors) may opt to initially straddle two jobs, keeping their civil service posts

Table 5:07. African Countries by Population Per Midwife Ratio

	Population Per Midwife	Countries
1 Chad,	1 per 20.000	Angola, Burkina Faso, Central African Republic,
		Equatorial Guinea, Eritrea, Guinea, Mali, Niger, Sierra Leone.
2	1 per 10.000	Benin, Gambia, Mauritania, Senegal, Togo
3	1 per 5.000	Comoros Islands, Republic of Congo, Cote d'Ivoire, Guinea-Bissau, Uganda
4	1 per 2.000	Ghana, Lesotho, Namibia, Nigeria, Sao Tome and Principe, Seychelles, Tanzania, Zimbabwe

Source: WHO (2002): Estimates of Health Personnel-1998

while moonlighting on the side. Countries may also formally allow double-practice, even in government health facilities, as in Mozambique.

The proliferation of Non-Governmental Organizations (NGOs) in the 1900s certainly caused a discernable exodus of health workers from the government service, either as direct health providers, program managers, or consultants. NGO health projects attract a wide range of government health professionals since the pay is much better and the work is similar to that of the civil servants, hence very little retraining costs are needed.

5:04-THE AFRICAN BRAIN-DRAIN FACTOR

A brain drain is a situation whereby a country experiences a shortage in skilled manpower when people with such expertise migrate to other countries to utilize such skills for individual and societal development. The brain drain dilemma is having very devastating effects and impact on the economies of all third world countries and especially the African continent. To properly address this problem, the remote and immediate causes must be well analyzed and evaluated from the political, social, economic, cultural, financial and academic perspective.

The United Nations Development Program (UNDP) notes that in Africa, the loss of medical Doctor has been the most striking. At least 60% of Doctors trained in Ghana during the 1980s have left the country. The United Nations Economic Commission for Africa and the International Organization for Migrations (IOM) estimate that 27000 Africans left the continent for industrialized countries between 1960 and 1975. It is estimated that since 1990 at least 20,000 people leave the continent annually. United Nations experts estimate that between 1960 and 1975,some 27000 well educated Africans departed for the west. From 1975 to 1984,the number of emigrants rose to 40,000 per year, and reach 80,000 by 1987, and the numbers have since leveled off, with an estimated 20,000 professionals leaving Africa each year since 1990.

The African brain drain is intimately linked with the shortage of health workers in industrial countries, which is fueling the demand. In the USA it is estimated that 126,000 nursing posts are currently unfilled and that the shortage will hit 500,000 full-time equivalent staff in 2015. Canada has an immediate need of 16,000 nurses and an estimated shortfall of 59,000 to 113,000 nurses by 2011. In 2001, it was estimated that 15,000 nurses were recruited in the U.K. and that 35,000 more are needed by 2008. In Australia, 31,000 nursing vacancies are expected by 2006. In Zambia, out of more that 600 doctors trained in the country since independence, only 50 remain. In Zimbabwe, out of 1200 doctors trained in the 1990s, only 360 are reported to be practicing domestically. In Sudan, an estimated 17 percent of physicians and dentists trained locally left in the 1980s and 1990s. Ghana, which has built a reputation for producing international-quality professional health workers, recorded a loss of 328 nurses from its Council of Nurses and Midwives' register in 1999.

Active foreign recruitment for health professionals, including x-ray technicians and radiographers, is ongoing in Ghana, Kenya, South Africa, Uganda, and Zambia through the local papers, professional journals, and job fairs. In 1998 an estimated 700 Ghanaian physicians are said to have been practicing in the USA alone that makes a considerable percentage of the population of Doctors in the country. It is estimated that about 20,000 Nigerians academics are now employed in USA alone and more than 300 Ethiopian physicians are working in Chicago, USA alone.

The financial ramifications of the brain on African economies are enormous. The United Nations Commission for Trade and Development has estimated that each migrating African professional represents a lost of $184000 to Africa, meanwhile Africa spends $4bn a year on the salaries of 100,000 or more on foreign professionals. Experts on the continent are increasingly engaged in strategies and programs to reverse the brain drain or retain skilled professionals at home. Organizations involved in repatriation face the challenge of attracting larger numbers of participants. The International Organization for Migration (IOM)'S re-integration of qualified African nationals program, which ran from 1983 to 1999, only managed to re-locate about 2000 nationals to 11 participating countries.

CHAPTER SIX

6:00- HEALTHCARE MANAGEMENT PROGRAMS IN AFRICA

Total Quality Management (TQM) is still a new management concept to most business organizations around the world and especially in the African continent. It implementation is more or less a paradigm shift because this requires total change in culture, attitude, organization, structure, operation, resource management and public relations.

In Africa, a lot of government and health services organizations are involved in the implementation of some quality improvement and management activities. But only a very of them are actually involved in this process. Only countries such as South Africa, Botswana, Malawi, Zimbabwe, Ghana, Nigeria, Cameroon, and Kenya have records of some quality management activities very active in their healthcare industries. However, quality assurance is just one component of the Total Quality Management concept because TQM involves a lot of many processes, changes and evolutions in culture, organization, lifestyle, attitude, operation, administration and the way the policies, goals and objectives as well as vision statement and philosophies of organizations are defined.

There are a couple of international organizations involved in the adoption and implementation of some quality management of a variety of healthcare programs in Africa. They are Advance Africa, Quality Assurance Project (QAP), John Hopkins Program (JHPIEG), The Population Council, and The Council of Health Service Accreditation in Southern Africa (COHSASA), the United States Agency for International Development (USAID), and the Center for African Family Studies (CAFS), The African Medical and Research Foundation (AMREF, the World Health Organization (WHO), African Council for Sustainable Health Development (ACOSHED), African Population and Health Research Center (APHRC), the West African Doctors and Healthcare Professionals Network (WADN), the African Networks for Health Research and Development (AFRO-NETS), the African Health Research Forum (AfHR) and the World Bank. But of their activities are limited to quality assurance and this is just a small component of the Total Quality Management process. There is then an absolute need for the introduction and implementation of the Total Quality Management concept in all these programs and various government and other institutions working towards the delivery of healthcare services in Africa.

6:01- PERFORMANCE IMPROVEMENT IN WEST AFRICA

In West Africa, the Santé Familial et Pré du SIDA (SFPS) project integrates both performance and quality improvement elements in its multi-agency collaborative approach. SFPS is a regional performance-based reproductive health project funded by USAID and implemented by four Cooperating Agencies. Target countries include: Burkina Faso, Côte d'Ivoire, Cameroon and Togo. SFPS intervenes and measures performance on both the provider and client side of the family planning (FP) service equation. The quality of provider performance (how competently and efficiently people are doing their work) contributes to reaching more clients. Improvements in quality of care attract, maintain and accommodate more FP clients in the program. The SFPS project has inherently followed the six-step performance improvement process.

1) Performance Analysis:

SFPS has designed a quality of care diagnostic tool that measures the quality of family planning services at healthcare delivery sites by examining 66 criteria. Data are collected through interviews with clients and providers, observation of clinical practice, and review of site management and logistics procedures. Gaps between actual and desired quality performance are identified and analyzed.

2) Root Cause Analysis:

Causes of performance and equality gaps are broadly grouped to include clinical knowledge and skill deficits among healthcare providers, low demand for family planning services, stemming from knowledge and awareness gap, weak management/logistics capacity (little control over procurement, planning, and budgets), low motivation caused by inadequate and irregular pay and weak communication and counseling skills of healthcare providers

3) Intervention Selection:

Based on the cause analysis, action plans are designed and interventions from five major categories are strategically applied such as service delivery, training and social marketing

4) Information, Education and Communication (IEC)::

Development and printing of IEC materials for service providers and clients, development of training programs to address communication and weaknesses in service delivery and outreach, and the development of mass media campaigns that promote and model positive health behaviors.

Rewards and Recognition: Establishment of an accreditation model through which sites that meet the quality criteria are declared Gold Circle sites. The surrounding community is then mobilized to further promote the use of services provided in the Gold Circle sites. The quality of work service providers to keep providing high standard work.

5) Implementation:

The operations research component of the project is responsible for monitoring the impact of the interventions and continuously providing feedback for qualitative and quantitative program improvement. This component aims at improving efficiency and effectiveness by diagnosing service delivery problems, testing performance improvement strategies and proposing solutions.

6) Monitoring and Evaluation of Performance:

In the first four years of the project SFPS succeeded in upgrading quality of care and motivating service providers. This has led to a greater use of family planning services. Couple years of Protection (CYP) generated by the 206 participating sites have steadily increased each year since 1995 and have exceeded expectations each year.

6:02- THE ADVANCE AFRICA PROJECT

Advance Africa is developing an integrated, process-oriented approach to service delivery management called Performance Monitoring Plus. Performance Monitoring Plus focuses on creating monitoring and information systems that capture the priority health intervention needs and desires of a given community. Advance Africa major activities towards quality improvement are:

1) Diversifying Service Delivery Mechanisms:

Advance Africa is committed to working with the health sector to improve family planning/reproductive health (FP/RH) services. Collaboration with existing non-health organizations and networks offers Advance Africa an important means of strengthening FP/RH services for individuals, groups, and communities.

2) Education:

Collaboration with the Forum for African Women Educationalists (FAWE), in Advance Africa consortium member, has provided an important mechanism for preventing unwanted pregnancies and sexually transmitted infections among adolescents.

3) Faith-Based Initiatives:

Religious leaders and faith-based organizations are often involved in the provision of health care in sub-Saharan Africa. Advance Africa works with these partners to strengthen FP/RH service delivery and health-seeking behavior.

4) Microfinance and Micro enterprise:

Advance Africa works with groups and networks to reach low-income populations in order to assist with income generation, information sharing, and behavior change.

5) Working with the Private Sector:

Many private sector instructions can help provide FP/RH commodities and services. Such private sector entities range from those selling condoms and oral contraceptives to those providing health services for employees.

6) Designing and Implementing Family Planning Services:

Advance Africa strives to address these issues for FP/RH services by:

- Enhancing the effectiveness of family planning at the program level
- Integrating family planning into other important health services, including HIV/AIDS services, post abortion care, and material and child health programs,
- Working with promising non-health sectors including faith-based groups, education, and micro enterprise systems,

- Focusing on the health benefits of birth spacing for mothers and children,
- Strategic mapping: a participatory approach to identifying successes, needs, and gaps in existing programs,
- Identifying best practices used by others that, when adapted to the new context, will successfully address unmet need and increase family planning demand, access, and use,

Advance Africa collaborates with local institutions, both public and private at both the national and community levels. It works to assess, design, and implement service delivery programs that effectively and efficiently meet the needs of individuals.

7) Strengthening Management Capacity:

Advance Africa works with country partners to improve and strengthen the management capacity of Ministry of Health facilities, nongovernmental organizations, and other local agencies, particularly at service delivery points such as clinics. Through training, planning, supervision, and monitoring and evaluation, we strive to assess strengths and weaknesses and build capacity for the highest quality of reproductive health services.

8) Performance Monitoring Plus:

This comprehensive approach to service delivery links monitoring and information systems with community needs, and aims to continuously improve provider performance.

9) Management Training:

With the Center for African Family Studies (CAFS), an Advance Africa consortium member, we provide training in multiple management topics to foster more effective and efficient service delivery.

10) Supervision:

At all levels, supervision of staff provides an opportunity for informal training, support, and qualitative monitoring.

Improving Family Planning through Management Training:

Service providers and program managers must work to acquire and strengthen their knowledge, attitudes, and skills-both clinical and managerial-through an effective training strategy that includes:

- Quality supervision,
- Performance monitoring,

- Human resources management,
- Program development,
- Budgeting and accounting.

Some of Advance Africa implementation structures are:

1) Management Sciences for Health:

Management Sciences for Health (MSH) seeks to increase the effectiveness, efficiency, and sustainability of health services by improving management systems, promoting access to services, and influencing public policy. As the prime contractor for the Advance Africa project, MSH provides:

- Financial and administrative expertise, as well as technical capacity in the education of health cares managers and providers,
- The application of practical management skills to public health problems in the public and private sectors,
- The strengthening of the technical, management, and leadership capabilities of individuals and institutions through collaborative work and training programs,
- The application and replication of innovations in health management.

2) The Centre for African Family Studies:

The Center for African Family Studies (CAFS) is an African institution dedicated to strengthening the capacity of organizations and individuals working to improve the quality of life of families in sub-Saharan Africa through family planning and reproductive health programs. To achieve this mission, CAFS conducts training courses and consultancies tailored to respond to specific needs; subjects include advocacy, behavior change communication, HIV/AIDS, gender and empowerment, management and leadership, youth reproductive health, and population development.

3) The Forum for African Women Educationalists:

The Forum for African Women Educationalists (FAWE) is an African network that works to ensure that African girls have access to schooling, complete their education, and have help to perform well at all levels. FAWE consists of 33 national chapters. The organization's overriding goal is to eradicate gender disparities in education by influencing the transformation of educational systems in Africa. FAWE advocates for girls and women's empowerment through education for girls, gender sensitivity and educational linkages, health and other policy reforms to advance community development, and women's rights.

4) The Academy for Educational Development:

The Academy for Educational Development (AED) is committed to solving critical social problems in the United States and around the world through education, social marketing, research, training, policy analysis, and innovative program design and management. Major areas of focus include health, education, youth development, and gender issues.

5) The Centre for African Family Studies (CAFS):

CAFS's comprehensive training approach builds upon CAF's expertise and is enhanced by the experience of other consortium members. It relies primarily on the knowledge and the expertise of high-level African trainers who provide both the technical assistance and the cultural capital needed to build a training program that is both technically sound and relevant to the local context.

6) Deloitte Touché Tohmatsu Emerging Markets:

Deloitte Touché Tohmatsu Emerging Markets (DTTEM) brings private sector strategies to the health sector in developing countries to maximize scarce resources and improve efficiency, quality, and institutional capacity. DTTEM expands the role of nontraditional private sector organizations, including private health providers, nongovernmental organizations, community-based organizations, and for-profit organizations, through facilitating innovative partnerships that leverage the comparative strengths and resources of each to improve public health.

6:03- THE QUALITY ASSURANCE PROJECT IN AFRICA (QAP)

The Quality Assurance Project (QAP) is funded by the U.S Agency for International Development (USAID) and its primary goal is to improve the quality of health, power and nutrition through state-of-the art technical support. QAP builds on over tend years of experience using modern quality assurance methods to improve healthcare in middle income and developing countries. QAP also addresses human resource management issues that impact quality of care and has been operating in many countries in the African continent with very positive results.

The Republic of Eritrea:

The Quality Assurance Project has been working in Eritrea since 1998 and primarily involved in the:

(1) Institutionalization of quality assurance (QA) within k programs of the Ministry of Health,

(2) Development of quality standards for hospitals and strengthening of the regulatory frames for improving the quality of healthcare, and

3) Improvement of human resource management and workforce development.

4) Improve management and quality of healthcare services provided by hospitals through standards development and in service training in quality management, infection prevention Emergency Triage Assessment and Treatment (ETAT),

5) Develop an improvement package for care of young children serious infections and severe malnutrition in all Pediatric hospital services refining/adapting guidelines of care for serious infection and severe malnutrition,

The Republic of Rwanda:

In Rwanda, the Quality Assurance Project is participating in the development quality improvement collaborative regarding treatment procedures and services for HIV/AIDS, Malaria, and Essential Obstetric care.

Some QAP activities in Rwanda include:

• Implement a national (Prevention of Mother-to-child-Transmission of HIV) PMTCT/Plus improvement collaborative 15 sites involving ten partners.

• Implement a malaria case management improvement collaborative involving four districts

• Implement an Essential Obstetric Care Improvement Collaborative in two districts

• Provide technical assistance to the Central Hospital of Kigali improve care of the Internal Medicine Department

• Provide technical assistance and training to the DPQS to develop the QA capacity of MOH

The Republic of Tanzania:

The Quality Assurance Project is working with the MOH and participating hospitals to establish an Infection Prevention Collaborative among the three district hospitals in the region of Dar es Salaam. The project will apply the

WHO/AFRO Policies and Guidelines for Infection Prevention development. The QAP activities in the Republic of Tanzania are:

- Introduce the collaborative improvement approach in resource poor settings to improve infection prevention practices
- Introduce WHO guidelines for infection prevention to the major theatre, minor theatre, and labor and delivery areas of the hospitals
- Establish infection control committees in each hospital
- Introduce quality improvement methods in each participating hospital department
- Assess the state of health worker stigma at the program hospitals at the end of one year
- Develop job aids around infection prevention topics
  Conduct a study of health worker stigma related to HIV/AIDS

The Republic of Malawi:

Major QAP activities in the Republic of Malawi are:
- Assist the National Quality Assurance Task Force (NQATF) to develop a national Quality Assurance policy and work plan for integrating a structure to support QA into the MOH structure
- Assist the NQATF to conduct an inventory of standards of care needed to implement the MOH's Essential Health Package
- Implement a pediatric hospital care improvement collaborative with district-level hospitals

The Republic of Niger:

The Quality Assurance Project is working with Niger's Ministry of Health to introduce a collaborative approach to pediatric activities in first-referral hospitals. The collaborative project is a joint effort with World Health Organization's country officers.

Major QAP activities: in the Niger Republic include:

- Adapt tools and assess the quality of pediatric hospital acre based on the WHO guidelines for first-referral hospitals
- Develop and implement a collaborative approach with 18 reference hospitals in 12 districts to improve case management for children under five years old

The Republic of South Africa:

The Quality Assurance Project (QAP), has been working in South Africa on accreditation hospitals, focused accreditation of youth-friendly services, and improving the quality of Maternal and Child Health (MCH), Tuberculosis, and HIV services in selected districts of Mpumalanga Province since 1999. QAP is also working to improve compliance with evidence based guidelines for such high-priority clinical services as HIV, PM, Tuberculosis, and Maternal and Neonatal Care. Significant QAP assistance in the Republic of South Africa centers on:

- Institutionalizing quality assurance system at various levels of health system in the Mpumalanga, KwaZulu-Natal, Limpopo, Eastern Cape, and North West provinces.
- Developing and implement training in quality methodology, including quality control (standards and monitoring), problem solving, and design, targeting priority clinical services, including HIV, STI, TB, maternal and child health
- Assisting Provincial Departments of Health to improve compliant with standards of care for priority clinical services through job aids, refresher training, process redesign, and team-based quality improvement
- Assisting the National Department of Health in identifying and communicating "best practices" through occasional symposia newsletters

6:04- THE JOHN HOPKINS PROGRAM FOR INTERNATIONAL EDUCATION IN GYNECOLOGY AND OBSTETRICS (JHPIEGO)

The John Hopkins Program in International Education Gynecology and Obstetrics (JHPIEGO) is an affiliate of John Hopkins University in Baltimore, Maryland, USA. In Africa, it works in close partnership with universities, ministries of health, and non-governmental organizations. Its dynamic partnerships help us address the needs of host-country partners to establish a national capacity to educate, train and support healthcare personnel to provide high quality services.

Its initiatives in Africa build on our core strengths, which are:

- Promoting pre-service education and in-service training as the keys to ensuring a continuous supply of health professionals with essential healthcare knowledge and skills
- Developing and disseminating healthcare guidelines at the national level
- Strengthening performance improvement throughout the healthcare delivery system
- Using innovative learning and training technologies to support a global network of faculty and trainers

- Creating practical, low-cost solutions to problems limiting the deliver of quality healthcare services
- Advocating for sound health policy

Currently, JHPIEGO has programs in 15 countries, maintains 2 sub-regional offices in Kenya and Cote d'lvoire, and 7 country offices in Burkina Faso, Cameroon, Ghana, Togo, Malawi, Uganda, and Zambia. JHPIEGO's programs in Africa focus on the following technical applications:

1) Reproductive Health:

JHPIEGO's work concentrates on strengthening the performance of healthcare providers through education and training in family planning, helping women and their partners avoid unwanted pregnancies, space births, and protect against sexually transmitted infections, including HIV/AIDS. These programs aim at improving the accessibility and quality of services for potential clients currently in Burkina Faso, Guinea, Haiti, Malawi, Senegal, and Zambia.

2) Post-abortion care:

The primary objectives of JHPIEGO's post-abortion care programs are to establish post-abortion care services, and/or expand post-abortion care services to increasingly decentralized sites. JHPIEGO has post-abortion care programs in Burkina Faso, Guinea, Haiti, Malawi, Senegal, and Zambia.

3) Infection Prevention:

Strengthening infection prevention practices is a component of JHPIEGO's programs in the region. JHPIEGO has programs that specifically focus on strengthening infection prevention in Burkina Faso, Haiti and Malawi.

4) Maternal and Neonatal Health:

JHPIEGO provides technical assistance and expertise in the areas of clinical services training and support, behavior change and social mobilization, and policy development. JHPIEGO has maternal and newborn health programs in Burkina Faso, Haiti, Tanzania, and Zambia.

5) Malaria in Pregnancy:

JHPIEGO is one of principal partners in WHO's and USAID's anti-malaria initiative, specifically focusing on the prevention and control of malaria during pregnancy. JHPIEGO has activities in Burkina Faso, Senegal, Tanzania, Uganda and Zambia, as well as regional initiative throughout the continent.

6) Cervical Cancer Prevention:

In Ghana, JHPIEGO has initiated a demonstration project designed to rigorously assess the safety acceptability, feasibility and programmatic effectiveness of cervical cancer prevention through the use of visual inspection with acetic acid and cryotherapy.

7) HIV/AIDS and Sexually Transmitted Infections:

JHPIEGO implements the service delivery and training components in the SFPS (Santé Familiale, Prevention du Sida) Its projects focus on Burkina Faso, Cameroon, Cote d'Ivoire and Togo.

6:05- THE COUNCIL OF HEALTH SERVICE ACCREDITATION IN SOUTHERN AFRICA (COHSASA).

COHSASA is the main agency responsible for setting standards for quality improvement and management of health care services in Southern Africa. It also enforces regulatory compliance by health institutions in the region. The underlying philosophy of the standards is based on principles of quality management and continuous equality improvement and aims to accommodate legal and ethical aspects. The standards can be used to guide the efficient and effective management of a healthcare organization and guide the organization and delivery of patient care services, and efforts to improve the quality and efficiency of those services.

In implementing its projects, COHSASA has taken into account the feedback from over 300 public and private facilities that have participated in its programs, the comments of its field staff, as well lay public with whom it comes into contact. COHSASA has a formal policy to review and, if necessary, to update its standards at regular, prescribed intervals. The current standards have been devised according to a set of principles developed by the International Society for Quality in Health Care (ISQua), in collaboration with over forty countries, to guide the content and structure of accreditation standards for hospital. International Society of Quality Assurance (ISQUA) has officially recognized COHSASA's sixth edition of Standards for Hospitals.

COHSASA's standards were set for each specific managerial, clinical and support service based on essential functions, and the current standards are organized around the important functions common to all healthcare organizations. Its standards also provide guidance to clinical services in order to give hospitals as much assistance as possible to meet the intention of the standards. The standards are organized into the following sections:

- Health Care Organization and Management
- Patient Care (including diagnostic and pharmaceutical services)
- Standards that focus on management of the organization address leadership of the organization, roles and responsibilities of staff, management of information, creation and maintenance of a safe environment for patients, infection prevention and control, quality of management and human resource management.

COHSASA has set standards that are service-specific and define the specific requirements of individual services, e.g. infection control in laundries, radiation protection in radiology departments, etc. Standards that relate to the effective and efficient management of HIV/AIDS in patients across the continuum of care have been incorporated into COHSASA has developed and tested a set of standards for the measurement of the efficacy of district HIV and AIDS services, using this approach, each service in a district is assessed against a common set of district standards covering the continuum of care provided to HIV+ patients.

COHSASA's Training Programs:

COHSASA facilitators or subcontracted consultants provide training throughout the program. The amount of training in these specialized fields varies depending on the needs of individual facilities. The major areas of training are:

1) Training in Quality Assurance Improvement:

COHSASA was developed as an accrediting organization that saw it as principally carrying out evaluations of health facilities against agrees standards.

The continuous quality assurance/improvement (CQI) approach was chosen as a tool to assist hospitals in their quest to achieve compliance with the program's standards. This CQI approach is taught to healthcare facility steering committees and to the small teams of the service areas/departments and it is aimed at applying the theory of CQI to address high-priority problems identified in baseline survey reports.

2) The Clinical Audit Program:

This program has been introduced into COHSASA's accreditation program as an integral part of the Continuous Quality Improvement (CQI) initiative to assist participating healthcare facilities to improve their clinical performance. The aim is to improve the quality of patient care, educate and train clinicians, make the best use of resources, and to improve service organization. The methods used in this program include a systematic measurement of current practice, followed by reference to research-based standards and the introduction of practical mechanisms for change, indicators, collaborative care pathways, and criterion-based topic audit.

3) *Training in Health and Safety:*

COHSASA's occupational health specialist has developed training program to cover topics such as employee and patient Safety, First Aid, Occupational Hazards etc.

4) *Training in Infection Control:*

Infection control is an area that presents great problems to healthcare facilities. COHSASA provides specialist training at workshops and a consultation service is available for special problems.

6:06- THE POPULATION COUNCIL

The Population Council carries out various activities in Sub-Saharan and other parts of the African continent to improve on the delivery of healthcare services. It focuses on improving the availability and the quality of contraceptive and reproductive health services and reducing the transmission of HIV/AIDS.

In Kenya, the Population Council has been involved in 'safe motherhood' activities and these include providing technical assistance for updating standards and national guidelines for essential obstetric care and undertaking innovative research with the Ministry of Health to test new approaches to providing safe motherhood services. The anticipated outcomes of these activities are to improve the quality of antenatal, delivery, postnatal, and post-abortion care services. The goal is also geared towards demonstrated effectiveness of systems of referral, access, health management, information, education, and communication services.

In Burkina Faso, the Council works with the government, the Burkina be Association for Family Welfare, the Mille Jeunes Filles project and the UNPF/UNICEF/UN Foundation to strengthen the social and health services to meet adolescent girls' health and developmental needs.

In Ethiopia, the Council works with the Family Guidance Association of Ethiopia on an operational research study to explore the impact of expanding the coital-dependent methods of family planning and emergency contraception.

The Population Council undertook a situational analysis in the Republic of Cameroon in 189 health services in order to improve the quality of family planning, child survival, and reproductive health services. It did so by evaluating the quality and efficiency of available services, developing methods to evaluate the quality and efficiency of maternal and child health/family planning program performance, and providing baseline data that could be used to evaluate the effects of AIDS interventions. The analysis revealed the need for improvement in the quality of clinic services, professional in-service training, providing necessary materials fro services, making staff more accountable to their services, and the need to reorganize and restructure some of the medical services.

In Ghana, the Population Council examined the association between social organization and reproductive behavior and the analysis revealed a weaker than expected association between the social organization of the communities and key reproductive indicators (fertility preferences, age at first marriage, postpartum practices, use of modern contraception). The Council has also helped to develop research systems, build research capacity and launch a research dissemination project at the research station of the Ministry of Health in Northern Ghana.

The activities of the Population Council in South Africa focus on clinical trials of Council-developed microbicide, operations research with mine workers, and workshops sharing study findings on how to reduce the stigma and discrimination against people living with HIV/AIDS. The Council's Frontiers in Reproductive Health program studied the feasibility and cost-effectiveness of improving public health clinic services for antenatal clients and the results showed a high demand for HIV testing and counseling. The Council assisted in the design of studies for the Nelson Mandela's Children's Goelama project and Development Research Africa. It also completed a baseline survey to assess the knowledge and attitudes of orphaned and vulnerable children concerning sexual and reproductive health. The Population Council also supports the Carletonville STI/HIV project and collaborates with the Council of Scientific and industrial Research, the South African Institute of Medical Research, and Family Health International/Impact on activities aimed at reducing the prevalence of sexually transmitted infections (STIs) and HIV incidences.

6:07- THE UNITED STATES AGENCY FOR INTETRNATIONAL DEVELOPMENT IN AFRICA (USAID)

The United States Agency for International Development is involved in a number of activities in some African countries to improve on the delivery of health care services such as Population and Family Planning, Child Survival, and HIV/AIDS Prevention and Mitigation.

In the Population and Family Planning program, USAID's objectives are to contribute to sustained and broad based economic growth by:

• Reducing the rapid rate of population growth through sustainable reduction in unintended pregnancies,
• Increasing the use of voluntary practices by women and men that contribute to the reduction of fertility,
• Improving maternal and child health by enabling women to space between births and limit family sizes,
• Relieving the stresses placed on employment, education and health care systems caused by rapid population growth.

In order to accomplish these objectives, USAID's priorities and activities are centered on increasing access to and demand for family planning services, encouraging greater involvement of NGO's, improving the quality of services and supporting extended access to education. Child Survival in Africa is another area where USAID is trying to make some improvements through reducing morbidity and mortality in the under-five population, strengthening health systems, and strengthening the capacities of African institutions. Its priorities and activities include:

• Support for health reform,
• Fostering partnerships between ministries of health and NGOs and commercial private sectors,
• Continued successful implementation of basic child survival intervention,
• Supporting the eradication of polio in coordination with WHO/AFRO and other partners.

One of USAID's major health programs in Africa is on HIV/AIDS prevention and mitigation. Its framework and principles are to increase policymaker's awareness of the impact of HIV/AIDS on their societies, focus on the prevention of infection, create sustainable programs, and emphasize continual program monitoring and evaluation.

6:08- CENTER FOR AFRICAN FAMILY STUDIES (CAFS)

The International Planned Parenthood Federation-Africa Region (IPPF-AR) founded the Center for African Family Studies in 1975. It is focused on strengthening the capacities of organizations and individuals working in the field of reproductive health, population and development in order to contribute to improving the quality of life of families in Sub-Saharan Africa.

CAFS major activities are centered on training, research, technical assistance, conference and consultancy, and partnerships and networking. It conducts operational research, community diagnosis, surveys and participatory rapid appraisals in Sexual and Reproductive health using qualitative and quantitative methods. It also provides short and long-term technical assistance I n both Francophone and Anglophone Sub-Saharan African countries in program design, management, implementation, monitoring and evaluation and institutional capacity building.

The Center for African Family Studies works with national, regional and international organizations such as partners in Population and Development, WHO, USAID and International Training Center of Tunis. It conducts and provides research and consultancy services from strategically located bases in East and West Africa with headquarters in Nairobi-Kenya, and a regional office in Lome-Togo.

6:09- THE AFRICAN MEDICAL AND RESEARCH FOUNDATION (AMREF)

The African Medical and Research Foundation's ultimate goal is to improve the health conditions of the disadvantaged population in the African continent suffering from a variety of health problems. Its priority activities focus on HIV/AIDS, tuberculosis, environmental sanitation, family health, clinical outreach, disaster and emergency management, and the development of health learning materials. The Foundation's strategy to accomplish these goals is capacity building, operational research and advocacy. AMREF emphasizes the development, testing and evaluation of systems that that are appropriate, relevant, effective and efficient.

The Flying Doctor Service operated by the foundation provides air evacuation services in emergencies as well as ambulance transfers between facilities and patient are flown to Europe and the USA. This service covers Eat Africa and neighboring northeast, south and central African countries.

6:10- THE WORLD HEALTH ORGANIZATION IN AFRICA

In Africa, the World Health Organization has promoted and disseminated the framework for a cyclical continuously improving approach to services management and quality assurance in the healthcare industry through its regional offices in collaboration with executive agencies such as the International Society of Quality Assurance (ISQUA), the Quality Assurance Project (QAP) French Cooperation and USAID. It also provides technical assistance for national capacity building in countries involved in the promotion and implementation of quality assurance and improvement programs and national accreditation efforts such as South Africa. WHO responds to requests from countries wishing to implement Quality Assurance and Improvement or Accreditation services and collaborates with development partners and NGO's, analyses and evaluates outcomes in national and regional events for their impact on health service delivery.

WHO works within the family of UNAIDS Cosponsors to facilitate multi-sensory efforts within the United Nations system. As part of its broad health-sector mandate in HIV/AIDS, it specially serves as the convening agency within the United Nations system for HIV/AIDS treatment, care and support as well as for preventing the mother-to-child transmission of HIV. WHO works closely with the UNAIDS Secretariat and Cosponsors at the global level and in countries with corresponding agencies through the United Nations country theme groups on HIV/AIDS. The roles WHO will perform as described here are consistent with whose overall mandate and the expectations expressed by the Organization's partners at a meeting in Geneva, Switzerland in May 2004. These include: -

- Support and advisory role with health ministries and national governments,
- Convening and coordinating partner efforts in scaling up treatment, care and prevention
- Technical expertise
- Planning
- Strategic information management and reporting
- Global support for high quality drugs and diagnostics
- Operations research and learning through experience
- Assisting countries in mobilizing resources
- Advocating for a comprehensive response to HIV/AIDS
- Leveraging WHO's organizational capability, and
- Identifying gaps and seeking solutions

Although WHO will not necessarily lead activities in all cases, it plays a valuable role in monitoring these gaps and in identifying solutions and working with others-especially UNAIDS Cosponsors-to develop them. (Source: WHO HIV/AIDS Plan 2004–2005). In designing the framework for health system performance, WHO broke new methodological ground, employing a technique not previous for health systems. It compares each country's system to what the experts estimate to be the upper limit of what can be done with the level resources available in that country. It also measures what each country's system has accomplished in comparison with those of other countries. World Health Organization's assessment system was based on five indicators:

1) Overall level of population health,
2) Health inequalities (or disparities) within the population,
3) Overall level of health system responsiveness (a combination of patient satisfaction and how well the system acts),
4) Distribution responsiveness within the population (how well people of varying economic status find that they are served by the health system), and
5) The distribution of the heath system's financial burden within the population.

A WHO regional meeting on local population held in Cape Verde in September 1998 recommended the facilitation of information exchange, regional and inter-country collaboration, improvement in manufacturing practices and inspectorate services also establishing regulatory tools to regulate production. The WHO aims to reduce morbidity from common illnesses by collaborating with countries to develop and implement national drug policies and programs, which ensure equal access to good quality essential drugs and their rational use. However, this requires new attitudes and new approaches to pharmaceutical sector issues. New challenges are emerging in several areas and these include:

1) Availability of financial resources,
2) Technical efficiency,
3) The role of the private sector,
4) Quality of health services,
5) Rational use of drugs, and
6) Regulation and quality assurance.
7) Increasing poverty, currency fluctuations, emerging new diseases, resistance to existing therapeutic agents, and irrational drug use are all putting more pressure on already constrained drug budgets.

To assist Member States in addressing priority issues, the WHO Regional Office for Africa is intensifying the activities of its Essential Drugs Program for Africa. This is an initiative, which seeks to build on ongoing activities in the Region, and encompasses five major components over a period of five years:

Component 1: Capacity building in drug regulation and quality assurance.
Component 2: Information exchange to improve policy implementation.
Component 3: Improving drug supply systems for health care.
Component 4: Improving rational drug use by prescribers, dispensers and the public.
Component 5: Building institutional capacity in Africa.

The above proposal has aims and objectives at both regional and country levels. WHO intends to implement it in collaboration with other interested partners over a five-year period? Within these five components some activities are already underway such as:

• Bulk purchasing of essential drugs by four West African States,
• Publication of the first edition of the AFRO Essential Drugs Price—Indicator and the AFRO Pharmaceuticals Newsletter,
• Creation of African Drug Regulatory Authorities Network (AFDRAN), and
• A comparative analysis of drug supply systems is in progress.

Support and commitment of the proposal by all Member States of the Region is integral to enable the Regional Office to raise funds. Once controlled by individual's governments, the Region's pharmaceutical sector is now opening to private sector initiatives. This is necessary for improving efficiency without compromising public health objectives.

6:11- AFRICAN POPULATION AND HEALTH RESEARCH CENTER (APHRC)

The African Population and Health Research Center (APHRC) were created to promote the wellbeing of Africans through research on population and health. In order to achieve these goals the center implements some degree of quality at all levels of research and reports are published in various leading scientific journals in order to facilitate the utilization of research results for improvement by making them available to policy makers and program managers.

The Center's goal is to contribute to the African scientific community through the publication of quality research papers in population, health and development. One outstanding feature of this center is its comprehensive and ethical review process, which requires all research products to be subject to internal and external reviews and in accordance with national and international ethical review procedures. The center also accentuates on the need for continuous dialogue with policy makers in disseminating research results as well as designing and implementing its projects. The center organizes technical workshops to enhance the skills of African scholars by exposing them to cutting edge theoretical, analytical and methodological issues on health, population and development research.

As part of its quality initiative, the APHRC maintains strong collaborative linkages between African and other international academic and research organizations such as the University of Pennsylvania, University of Maryland, University of Southampton, and the Population Council, PATH, CARE and JHPIEG at John Hopkins University. APHRC is also a member of INDEPTH, an international network of field sites conducting continuous demographic surveillance of populations aimed at generating reliable health information to improve policy and research in poor nations.

6:12- AFRICAN COUNCIL FOR SUSTAINABLE HEALTH DEVELOPMENT (ACOSHED)

The African Council for Sustainable Health Development was created to promote African ownership of health development, encourage quality management and improve the performance of healthcare systems. Its mission is to advocate for improved health governance and assist African governments and people in their efforts to reform health policy, establish secure health systems and integrate health into overall poverty reduction programs and socio-economic development of all communities.

ACOSHED informs and educate the public, opinion leaders, the media and policy-makers about critical issues in global health and the need for appropriate investment and actions to address these problems. In order to accomplish this goal, it organizes regular educational briefings on Capitol Hill, plans for Congressional study tours and hosts consultation meetings with organizations such as the World Health Organization and the World trade Organization on differential pricing and the financing of essentials drugs.

6:13- WEST AFRICAN DOCTORS AND HEALTHCARE PROFESSIONALS NETWORK (WADN)

The West African Doctors and Healthcare Professionals Network is a virtual group of experts interested in improving the quality of healthcare service delivery in the West African Sub-region. It promotes information and knowledge exchange in the area of distance-learning, telemedicine and knowledge support of diagnosis, treatment and management of the patient. This activities of this organization will certainly transform the practice of medicine not only in West Africa which it presently serve but across the entire African continent taking into consideration the effects and impact of cutting technology on the practice of modern medicine around the world.

6:14- THE AFRICAN HEALTH RESEARCH FORUM (AFHR)

The prime objective of the African Health Research Forum is to promote health research for development in Africa as a whole and projects focus on research ethics, leadership development and communication systems for sharing research information. This organization enhances the mechanisms for strengthening the conduct, collaboration and coordination of health research, promotes the utilization of research for development and strives to reduce the inter-country, regional and global imbalances in health research.

The ultimate goal of the African Health Research Forum is to develop leadership and management capacity in Africa for health research and knowledge production at community, national, regional and institutional levels. This could help to improve knowledge base and technical know-how, improve health service delivery, strengthening leadership skills in policy formulation and strategic planning, visionary leadership and good governance in health research. The Forum collaborates with WHO-AFRO and the African Advisory Committee for Health Research and Development (AACHRD) and other international organizations to provide guidance on improving and strengthening the capabilities for bioethics in health research in Africa.

6:15- AFRICAN NETWORKS FOR HEALTH RESEARCH AND DEVELOPMENT (AFRO-NETS)

The African Networks for Health Research and Development is an independent watchdog organization in the healthcare industry in Africa. It monitors health problems, policies, strategies and programs and advocates for resources and improved health policies for the continent. It accomplishes this goal through the auditing of international organizations involved in health research in Africa, assessing regional and national health policies and programs, monitoring the role of the private sector in healthcare service delivery, advocating for action on audited issues, promoting networking among health institutions, agencies and experts in Africa and advocating for institutional capacity building for local health institutions.

6:16- THE WORLD BANK AND HEALTHCARE IN AFRICA

THE World Bank and the International Monetary Fund finance a lot of social and infrastructural project in the Third World. But in the 1980's it introduced the Structural Adjustment Program (SAP) in most African countries seeking aid. This is a package of economic policies designed to fix imbalances in trade and government budgets. During this decade, African countries required essential investments in health, education, and infrastructure in order to compete internationally. The World Bank and the International Monetary Fund encouraged most third world countries to implement the SAP programs which were meant to provide temporarily financing to borrowing countries to stabilize their economies, integrate them into the global economy, strengthen the role of the international private sector and encouraged growth through trade. The main components of the Structural Adjustment Program included cutbacks in government spending, privatization of government enterprises and services, reduce protection for domestic industry, currency devaluation, increased interest rates, and elimination of food subsidies. Although the Structural Adjustment Programs varied in implementation from country to country, they all forced a lot of African countries to adopt very stringent austerity measures which had very devastating effects and impact in the health care sector in particular and other sectors of the economy. Some of these measures include:

A)- A shift from growing diverse food crops for domestic consumption to producing cash crops or other commodities for export,

B)- Abolishing food and agricultural subsidies to reduce government expenditures,

C)- Severe cuts to health, education and housing programs as well as massive cuts and layoffs in the civil service,

D)- Currency devaluation to make exports cheaper but imports more expensive,

E)- Liberalization of trade and investment, and increase in real interest rates to attract foreign investment,

F)- Privatization of government held enterprises and services.

These World Bank's Structural Adjustment Program reforms had a reverse effect on the health care systems in most African countries. Prior to its implementation, most district hospitals, community health centers and other outreach health posts provided medical services and essential drugs free of charge. With the reforms, user fees and cost recovery were introduced and the sale of drugs was liberalized. With the deregulation of the pharmaceutical industry and the liberalization of drug prices, imported branded drugs were sold in the free market at enormous costs thereby displacing domestic drugs. Most African governments were unable to provide budget support to health services and this paralyzed the public health system. The dramatic drop in health expenditures in 1980's and 1990's resulted in the closure of hundreds of clinics, hospitals and medical facilities across the continent. In Sub-Saharan Africa, the level of polio vaccination dropped by more than 10% as a result of cutbacks in health care services between 1990–1992. In Ghana the number of doctors in the government health care system dropped from 1700 to 665 and most of the left the country. This resulted in a medical professional brain drain and hundreds of thousands of medical doctors from Nigeria, Senegal, Ethiopia, Kenya, and Zimbabwe fled for better job opportunities in Europe and the USA.

Chapter Seven

7:00- HEALTHCARE SYSTEMS

A healthcare system is the organization by which an individual or group's health is being managed for an effective and efficient service delivery. It is usually a hospital system, an insurance company or a specific and specialized health institution.

In Africa, the commonest healthcare systems are the traditional health system made up of traditional doctors, soothsayers and fortune-tellers, and the modern hospital health systems. Meanwhile most African governments run state hospitals to help those who cannot afford for expensive health services offered by private hospitals. In the 1960's, 1970's and 1980's, consultation and medication in government hospitals was free and even hospitalization. But of late, people consult free and procure their medication at their expense. In case of hospitalization, they some pay a discharge fee. Of late a couple of countries such as Nigeria and Ghana have launched the National health Insurance Schemes to provide basic healthcare coverage to its citizens. In South Africa there is the Health System Trust as the dominant healthcare system striving to provide health services to the entire country. There are many private health insurance providers in most African countries rendering services to either their expatriate staffs or nationals working with these organizations. The provision of critical healthcare treatment in most African communities is based on the "ability-to-pay principle". This depends on whether the individual has the means to pay or whether some form of family resources exist to pay for the medical services that he or she has to receive. Healthcare professionals who are obligated by their oaths of service to protect consumers in any circumstance often find themselves in an ethical dilemma situation where they are sometimes obliged by economic and financial circumstances beyond their control to violate their oath by preferring money to rendering medical services. Health system provides the critical interface between life-saving life-enhancing interventions and the people who need them and if the health systems are weak as is the case with most African countries, then the power of these interventions is likewise weakened, or even lost.

Basic Healthcare systems models are:

Purely private enterprise healthcare systems are comparatively rare for a comparatively well-off subpopulation in a poorer country with for instance, private clinics for a small expatriate population in an of are countries with a majority private healthcare system.

The other major models are public insurance systems:

1) Social security healthcare model, where workers and their family contribute to the fund
2) National Health Service model, where the residents of the country are totally taken care by the government for example government hospitals and National Health Insurance.

7:01- HEALTHCARE SYSTEMS AROUND THE WORLD:

The majority of industrial societies have publicly funded health systems that cover the great majority of the population for example Medicare in Canada and Australia, Medicare and Medicaid in the United States.

The role of the government in healthcare provision is however a source of continued debate with diverges sharply. Even among countries that have publicly funded medicine, different countries have different approaches to the funding and provision of medicine. Some areas of difference are whether the system will be funded from general government revenues (e.g. Italy, Canada) or through a government system (France, Japan, Germany) on a separate budget and funded with special separate taxes. Another difference is how much of the cost of for by government or social security system, in Canada all hospital care is paid for by the government while in Japan patients must pay 10 to 20 dollars a hospital stay. What will be covered by the public system is also important, for instance, the Belgian government pays the bulk of the fees for care, while the Australian government covers neither.

In Australia the current system, known as Medicare, was instituted in 1984. It coexists with a private health system. Currently, the tax funding Medicare has lead to a severe revenue shortfall, with increased costs to patients. This has triggered reforms by the Howard scheme. Many critics claim that these reforms are in fact a move away from the principle of universal health care.

Canada has a federally sponsored publicly funded Medicare system, but each province may opt in or out but none currently do. Basic wholly public, with no fee for service allowed. Other areas of health care such as dentistry and optometry are almost wholly private. In Finland the publicly funded medical system is funded by taxation and every citizen has a state-funded health insurance. The system is comprehensive and compulsory, like in Sweden, and a small patient fee is also taken. In France, most doctors remain in private practice; there are both private and public hospitals. Social Security is a public organization of them) distinct from the state government, and with separate budgets. It generally refunds patients 70% of most health care costs, of costly or long-term ailments. Supplemental coverage may be brought from private insurers, most of them nonprofit, mutual insurance social security coverage was restricted to those who contributed to social security (generally, workers or retirees), excluding some patient populations, the government of Lionel Jospin put into place the "universal health coverage."

In Israel, the publicly funded medical system is universal and compulsory. Payment for the services are shared by labor unions, the.

In Sweden, the publicly funded medicine system is comprehensive and compulsory. Physician and hospital services take a small patient services are funded through the taxation scheme of the County Councils of Sweden

In 1948, the United Kingdom passed the National Health Service Act that provided free physician and hospital services to all citizens and nurses are on government payroll and receive salaries, a fixed fee for each patient assigned, and enhanced payments for specialized skills. The National Health Service has been amended from time to time, but is largely intact. Around 86% of prescriptions are provided. Prescriptions are provided free to people who satisfy certain criteria such as low income or permanent disabilities. People that pay full cost (average cost to the health service was 11.10-about 16.70, US $20.40—IN 2002). Funding comes from a hypothecated health from general taxation. Private health services are also available.

Almost every country that has a publicly funded health care system also has a parallel private system, generally catering to the wealthy. From the inception of the National Health Service model (NHS, 1948), public hospitals in the United Kingdom have included "amenity beds" which would typically be more comfortable and serve as private wards in some hospitals where for a fee more amenities is provided. These are predominantly used for surgical operations are generally carried out in the same operating theatres as the NHS work and by the same personnel. These amenity beds do not include socialized healthcare systems, like the Spanish one, among others. From time to time the NHS pays for private hospitals (arranged hospitals) surgical cases for which the NHS facility does not have sufficient capacity. The same doctors usually, but not always, do this work. Even in the United States healthcare for the elderly, also known as Medicare, is financed from taxation, but often provided by privately owned physicians in private practice. Another example is France where Social Security is a public entity, which refunds patients for care in both primary facilities; the majority of French doctors are in private practice. In some systems, patients can also take private health insurance, but choose public hospitals, if allowed by the private insurer. While the goal of public systems is to provide equal service, the egalitarianism is thus always partial. Every nation either has parallel private citizens are free to travel to nation that does, so there is effectively a two-tier healthcare system that reduces the equality of service. Since they are typically better paid, those medical professionals motivated by remunerative concerns migrate to the private sector while the private hospital has newer and better equipment and facilities.

A number of countries such as Australia attempt to solve the problem of unequal care by insisting their time between public and private systems. Proponents of these parallel private systems argue that they are necessary to provide flexibility to the system and are a way to increase funding care system as a whole by charging the wealthy more. Opponents believe that they are allowed to exist mainly because politicians and would prefer better care. They also argue that all citizens should have access to high quality healthcare. The only country not to have any private system for basic healthcare is Canada. However, many wealthy Canadians go to the United States for care. Also, in some cases, doctors are so well paid in both systems that prestige is often more important to them than remuneration. This is very evidenced in the United Kingdom where private medicine is seen as less prestigious than public medicine by much of the population. As a result, the best doctors spend the majority of their time working for the public system, even though they may also do some work for private healthcare providers. The British tend to use private healthcare to avoid waiting lists rather than because they believe that they will receive better care from it.

7:02- HEALTHCARE SYSTEMS IN AFRICA

Health care in Africa is both traditional (voodoo medicine) and western (modern medical) with the latter being managed by the government through the Ministries of Public Health. African traditional medicine has been around for centuries and Traditional Healers developed their health systems with the support of the communities. These individuals are sometimes regarded as "prophets" and develop their own healing traditions, ways of diagnosing, classifying and treating various illnesses as well as pricing. In the early times right to the 1950's there was often no monetary exchange for the treatment of any disease but family members of the patient could offer any gifts as token for appreciation for services rendered by the traditional healer. But from the 1960's because of the influence of western capitalism on the practice of medicine, there has been the proliferation of African traditional medicine clinics in the continent and this has now become a huge financial undertaking with charges in hundreds of thousands and even millions depending on the illness. At first traditional healers were said to be inspired by God and were looked upon as people who has received a special vocation to serve the sick. But nowadays, it is common to find crooks and unscrupulous individuals in most African communities opening up traditional healing clinics claiming that there are "messiahs" and "prophets" and advertising their services on billboards, television and newspapers.

The philosophy of African traditional medicine is centered on meta-physical causes and cures notably, influence of the gods, spirits, ancestors, witchcraft etc. The approach is holistic because the goal is to return the patient to his original social and cultural self. Herbal remedies remain the most popular form of medication for African traditional medicine. In the African traditional healing system there is a very strong bond and symbiotic relationship between the healer and the community. A resident healer may serve the entire community depending on the circumstances. Some may specialize as diviners, midwives, magicians, psychic readers etc.

Western medical system did not get into Africa until after the First World War. That is when early missionaries set up small clinics and health centers in West, Central and South Africa. Now the system is operated by government through a functional organizational structure under the ministry of health. The medical services trigger down to the provinces, divisions, subdivisions and districts. This approach focuses on the individual and the scientific methods of understanding the causes and effects of diseases. Financial, material and management problems plague most government health services and making more people to turn to traditional medicine.

It is worth noting that medical malpractice litigation is not very common in Africa as is in Europe and the United States. Medical professionals are seldom held accountable for any problems on patients as a result of their treatment. This plays a major role on the quality of practice as well their ability to be more assiduous and responsible to the patients they treat.

Some healthcare systems operating in some countries in Africa are:

7:02-01-South African Healthcare System

The transition from apartheid to democracy in 1994 with Nelson Mandela as the president saw some substantial changes in the separate health systems which had existed for decades where whites and blacks received separate medical treatment. The government now allocates about 15% of government expenditures to health infrastructure and services and its goal is to decrease mortality rates, HIV/AIDS infection rates, revitalize public health services, improve resource mobilization, management and equity in allocation, improve human resources development and management, hasten legislative reform, and strengthen cooperation with international partners. In 2003, the South African government approved the treatment plan for HIV and to distribute free AIDS medicine to anyone who needs it. The South African Department of Health is responsible for the management of the health system and its infrastructures.

The Republic of South Africa is the most developed in Africa now with a population of about 44 millions. The Department of Health is shifting to equitable access to health services through its Health Sector Strategic Framework which focuses on decreasing morbidity and mortality rates through strategic interventions, revitalization of public hospital services, acceleration of delivery of essential Primary Healthcare Services, improving resource mobilization and management of equity in allocation, improving human resources development and management, improving quality of care, enhancing communication and consultation in the health system and with communities, legislative reforms, re-organization of certain support services and the strengthening cooperation with international partners.

Health System Trust (HST) is the dominant healthcare agency in South Africa and its mission has been to develop a comprehensive, effective, efficient and equitable healthcare delivery system in the country. This is achieved through activities such as health system research, health system development, advocacy, and capacity development and information dissemination and through the implementation of programs such as Community Development, Health Link and the Initiative for Sub-District Support.

Health System Trust Research program focuses on Primary Health Care Facilities, Decentralization and District Health Systems, HIV/AIDS and Sexually Transmitted Diseases, Reproductive health, Maternal and Child Health, Human Resources and Support Systems for Health. The organization tries to improve on the quality of primary health care services through empowerment of clients and providers as well as support and facilitation.

Equity Gauge is a very important agency created by the Health System Trust as a lobbying organization with the South African legislators to promote equitable health and health care in the country. It main functions are to assess and monitor equity in health and health care, provide equity oriented information to legislators, analyze health policies with reference to budgeting and resource allocation, strengthen the accessibility of health data, empower and educate disadvantaged communities on their rights to health care and communicate the information to legislators. Equity Gauge is like a watchdog for health services in South Africa and Health System Trust effectively and efficiently collaborates with it in terms information exchange and program and activities identification and development.

The Council of Health Services Accreditation of Southern Africa (COHSASA) Sets policies and standards for the operation of health care services in the country. It is charged with monitoring and evaluating the activities and services of healthcare providers in Southern Africa. It undertakes performance evaluation of services to make sure that they meet certain legal, social, ethical, financial, educational and professional standards of operation.

Some renowned medical research institutions in South Africa are Aurum Health Research, the Global Alliance for TB Drug development, the Medical Research Council, the medical University of South Africa, the South African National Institute of Virology, the University of Cape Town and Natal Faculty of medicine and the University of Witwatersrand.

7:02-02- Healthcare System in Nigeria

The proliferation and marketing of traditional medicine clinics is becoming a major concern in the Nigerian healthcare industry, Traditional doctors open their clinics to the public and charges vary depending on the illness. This has become a major money making industry and their products and services are well marketed on TV and newspapers and billboards. It is worth noting that there is just no control over their products or services and the quality of their services and products to citizens remain a very big question to be answered.

Healthcare in Nigeria is generally provided by the Ministry of Health, which develops the policies and provides funding and technical support. Every state has a hospital with many Local Government Hospitals and health clinical. There are many private hospitals and clinics and tradition medicine (Voodoo) is well renowned and marketed as well. Nigeria has a lot of teaching hospitals and the most renowned are Port Harcourt, Enugu, Lagos, Ilorin and Jos. Many research institutions also operate with budget such as the Ahmadou Bello University teaching Hospital, Nigerian Institute of medical Research, Obefemi Awolowo College of Health Sciences, the University of Calabar and the University of Ibadan. The country also has many pharmaceutical industries such as the Evans Medical PLC, which is making some advances in the development of drugs with help form foreign partners.

The Nigerian government recently launched the National Health Insurance Scheme whose activities will be base on a system of care focusing on Primary health care, Secondary Health Care and Tertiary health Care. Its main functions are educating citizens on prevailing health problems, promotion of food supply and proper nutrition, maternal and child care, immunization, prevention and control of local epidemic and endemic diseases and the provision of essential drugs and other medical supplies.

This project is still in its infancy and yet to be implemented. But the mere launching is an optimistic approach to provide affordable healthcare to its citizens. A major deterrent will be the bureaucratic system, corruption, its population explosion of about 115 million inhabitants, a huge international debt and political crisis.

7:02-03- Aga Khan Health Services- East Africa

The Aga Khan Health Services began in the 1930's in Dar es Salaam in Tanzania and soon spread to Kenya and Uganda. It focuses on health system development, raising the health status of people through providing quality healthcare services. The Aga Khan Foundation and the Aga Khan University collaborate in the training of healthcare professionals especially nurses in order to facilitate the staffing of its various research projects. The foundation works with various governments in East Africa to develop tools for health sector policy design and resource allocation and works to assure the sustainability of existing health facilities operated by the Aga Khan Health Services.

7:02-04- Healthcare System in Cameroon

The healthcare delivery system in Cameroon is both public and private. The public health system is run through the Ministry of Health and related health institutions, which include 1 university teaching hospital, 2 reference hospitals and 10 provincial hospitals. Every division and sub-division has a hospital. The World Health organization estimates that Cameroon has 7.4 physicians and 36.7 nurses per 100.000 populations. Consultation and hospitalization with any government hospital in Cameroon is free but patients purchase their drugs.

Cameroon developed the National Strategic Plan Against AIDS whose activities are focused on prevention targeting youths and women, involvement of employees and religious organizations, condom distribution, blood supply safety and HIV surveillance.

Traditional medicine is very popular in Cameroon and affordable to many. Some traditional doctors charge a minimal fee, some don't. They may instead demand some material gifts in exchange for their services. Their medication is produced fro backs of trees, leaves and animals. Cameroon traditional medicine has attracted international researchers because of its reputation in the treatment of a variety of chronic illnesses.

Private healthcare is dominantly in the hands of big corporation such as the Cameroon Development Corporation (CDC), Pamol, Socapalm, etc. These corporations develop and run their own hospitals and clinics for their employees and families. Public corporations such as SANARA, BEAC,

CAMAIR, the National Social Insurance Fund etc all have health insurance schemes for their employees and families.

The main medical research institutions in Cameroon are the organization de Coordination pour la lutte contre les endemies en Afrique Centrale (OCEAC) and the School of medical Sciences (CUSS).

The Cameroon Ministry of Public Health recently launched the National Forum on Hospital Reforms in order to eradicate corruption in the healthcare system and address other issues such as malpractice by healthcare professionals, lack of material and financial resources, mismanagement, insufficient training and research and the inability of an average Cameroonian to obtain decent healthcare service in public hospitals. Another alarming issue is the very high "doctor-patient ratio" and "nurse-patient ratio" which negatively impact the quality of service delivery in healthcare facilities in the country. Various problems affecting health services in hospitals were analyzed and evaluated. These included corruption, poor organization, poor resource organization and management, lack of leadership, ethics violation by healthcare professionals and the general lack of communication at all levels. A Strategic Plan to Improve Cameroonian Hospitals was then adopted whose goal focus on the implementation of health development research, the reorganization of emergency services, making drugs available and affordable to patients, encouraging access to health services, upholding professional code of ethics, increased financing to health projects and human resource development and management through training.

7:02-05- Healthcare System in Ghana

Ghanaian healthcare is both public and private as any other African country. The country recently launched its National health Insurance Plan but it is still to be fully implemented. Public health services are provided through government hospitals at provincial and district levels. Ghana has 1 hospital bed per 638 populations, and 1 physician per 22,970 populations. The northern region of the country is disadvantaged in health resources as most of them are concentrated in the coastal areas especially around the capital city of Accra. Ghana's two prominent teaching hospitals are the Korle-Bu located in the capital and Komfo Anokye in Kumasi Some other major health research institutions in the country are the center for Tropical Clinical Pharmacology and Therapeutics, Navrongo health research center and the Noguchi Memorial Institute for Medical Research.

Faith-based Non-Governmental Organization represented by the Christian health Association of Ghana provides about 40% of the country's healthcare services. Traditional medical is also very popular especially in the northern region where there are limited public health facilities.

7:02-06- Healthcare System in Botswana

The healthcare system in Botswana is one of the best in Africa. Its public health system consists of 23 district health centers, 3 referral hospitals, 12 district hospitals, 17 primary hospitals, 222 clinics, 330 health posts and 740 mobile stops. Marina Hospital in the capital city of Gaborone is the largest healthcare facility in the country. The World health Organization estimates that Botswana has 23.8 physicians and 219.1 nurses per 100.000 populations.

7:02-07- Healthcare System in Tanzania

Tanzania's healthcare delivery system is mostly state-run and is designed with so many dispensaries providing most of the health care and making referrals to health centers, district hospitals, regional hospitals and referrals to hospitals run by large charitable organizations. There are 8 referrals hospitals, 17 regional hospitals, 68 district hospitals 102 provincial hospitals, 479 health centers and more than 3600 local dispensaries. The World health Organization estimates that Tanzania has 4.1 physicians and 85.2 nurses per 100.000 populations.

The main health research institutions in Tanzania are the Hubert Kairuki Memorial University, the African Malarial testing network, the Muhimbili University College of Medical Research, the national Institute of Medical Research and the Tanzanian Essential Health Intervention Project.

7:02-08- The Ethiopian Healthcare System

Ethiopia is one of the poorest countries in the world with a per capita income of $100 per year and a huge population of about 68 million inhabitants. For the past decades, its healthcare system has been negatively affected by war, drought and flooding, giving it one of the highest malnutrition rates in the world too.

The country now has three medical schools at the University of Addis Ababa, Jimma University and the College of Medical Sciences, a host of public hospital and many private hospitals and clinics.

The fundamental principles of Ethiopian healthcare system now focus on the democratization and decentralization of the health service system, development of the preventive and promotional components of healthcare, development of an equitable and acceptable standard of health service system that will serve all segments of the population within the limits of resources, promoting and strengthening of intersectional activities, promotion of attitudes and practice conducive to the strengthening of national self-reliant development and assurance of accessibility of health care for all segments of the population.

7:02-09- Healthcare System in Kenya

Kenya has one of the most developed healthcare systems in Sub-Saharan Africa but a great percentage still remains without access to good health services.

The country's health policy is implemented by the Ministry of Health and has been privatizing some health facilities since the late 1980's in order to makes services available to citizens. The country has about 3,200 health institutions and of this there are 1,100 dispensaries, 400 health centers, 100 hospitals and many Non-Governmental Organization and mission health institutions.

The main medical research institutions in Kenya are the Kenya Medical Research Institute, International Center for Insect Physiology and Ecology, Kenyan AIDS Vaccine Initiative, MOI University, the African Medical and Research Foundation, the United States Army Medical Research Unit and the University of Nairobi.

7:03-WORLD HEALTH ORGANIZATION AND HEALTHCARE SYSTEMS

The World Health Organization carries out various assessments of healthcare systems based on five indicators: -

1) Overall level of population health,
2) Health inequalities (or disparities) within the population,
3) Overall level of health system responsiveness (a combination of patient satisfaction and how well the system acts),
4) Distribution of responsiveness within the population (how well people of varying economic status find that they are served by the health system), and
5) The distribution of the health system's financial burden within the population (who pays the costs). Healthcare systems around the world are measured ranked according to the following criteria by the World Health organization:

1) Responsiveness:

The nations with the most responsive health systems are the United States, Switzerland, Luxemburg, Denmark, Germany, Japan, Canada, Norway, Netherlands and Sweden. The reason these are all advanced industrial nations is that a number of the elements of responsiveness depend strongly on the availability of resources. In addition, many of these countries were the first to begin addressing the responsiveness of their health systems to people's needs.

2) Fairness of financial contribution:

When the World Health Organization measures the fairness of financial contribution to health systems around the world, countries often line up differently. The measurement is based on the fraction of a household's capacity to spend (income minus food expenditure) that goes on health care (including tax payments, social insurance, private insurance and out of pocket payments). Columbia was the top-rated country in this category, followed by Luxembourg, Belgium, Djibouti, Denmark, Ireland, Germany, Norway, Japan and Finland.

3) Overall Level of Health:

A good health system, above all, contributes to good health. To assess overall population health and thus to judge well the objective of good health is being achieved, WHO has chosen to use the measure of Disability-Adjusted Life Expectancy (DALE) the advantage of being directly comparable to life expectancy and is readily compared across populations. The report provides estimates for countries of disability-adjusted life expectancy. DALE is estimated to equal or exceed 70 years in 24 countries, and 60 years in over half Member States of WHO. At the other extreme are 32 countries where disability-adjusted life expectancy is estimated to be less than 40 years. Many of these are countries characterized by major epidemics of HIV/AIDS, among other causes.

4) Distribution of health in the Populations:

It is not sufficient to protect or improve the average health of the population; if-at the same time inequality worsens or remains high because the gain accrues disproportional to those already enjoying better health. The health system has the responsibility to try to reduce inequalities by prioritizing actions to improve the health of the worse-off, wherever these inequalities caused by conditions amenable to intervention. The objective of good health is really twofold: the best attainable average level-goodness of the smallest feasible differences among individuals and groups-fairness.

5) Responsiveness:

Responsiveness includes two major components. These are (a) respect for persons (including dignity, confidentiality, and autonomy of individuals and families decide about their own health); and (b) client orientation (including prompt attention, access to social support networks during care, quality of basic amenities and choice of provider).

6) Distribution of Financing:

The objectives of the health system do not include any particular level of total spending either absolutely or relative to income. This is because, at all levels of spending there are other possible uses for the resources devoted to health. The level of funding to allocate to the health system is a social choice. In order to reflect these attributes, health systems have to carry out certain functions and build human resources through investment and training. Whatever standard is applied, it is evident that health systems in some countries perform well, while others perform poorly. This is not due to differences in income or expenditure. The way health systems are designed, managed and financed affects people's lives and likelihoods.

The difference between a way of performing health system and one that is failing can be measured in death, disability, impoverishment, humiliation and despair:

The ultimate responsibility for the performance of a country's health system lies with government and the careful and responsible management of the wellbeing of the population is the very essence of good government. The health of people is always a national priority: government responsibility for its continuous and permanent.

For the dollar for dollar spent on health, many countries are falling short of their performance potential. The result is a large number of preventable deaths and lives stunted by disability. The impact of this failure is born disproportionately by the poor.

Health systems are not just concerned with improving people's health but with protecting them against the financial costs of illness challenge facing governments in low income countries is to reduce the regressive burden of out-of-pocket payment for health by expanding prepayment schemes, which spread financial risks and reduce the specter of diastrophic health care expenditure. Within governments, many health ministries focus on the public sector often disregarding the frequently much larger-private finances and provision of care. A growing challenge is for governments to harness the energies of the private and voluntary sectors in achieving better levels of health systems performance, while offsetting the failures of private markets. Stewardship is ultimately concerned with oversight of the entire system, avoiding myopia, tunnel vision and the turning of a blind a system's failings.

7:04- TYPICAL HEALTHCARE SYSTEM DESIGN

Well-designed healthcare systems can create an environment in which the care of people living with disease can be more effective and efficient resulting in qualitative service delivery. Critical elements include a coherent approach to system improvement, leadership committed to and responsible for improving clinical outcomes, and incentives to providers and patients to improve care and adhere to guidelines such as:

1) Making Improving in Chronic Care a part of the Organization's vision, mission, goals, performance improvement, and business plans,
2) Linking HIV/AIDS disease care improvement, measures, and outcomes to the strategic business plan,
3) Gain the senior leader's interest with reports and feedback,
4) Providing senior leaders with data about the benefits of the initiative, including better results on patient satisfaction surveys and improved patient outcomes,
5) Have the team leader or physician champion regularly report progress and results to the Board.

7:04:01- Steps in Designing the System

Some fundamental principles to be considered when designing a healthcare system include:
  1) Describing and Documenting the New Delivery System:
  This involves:

- Mapping the current process and evaluating the gaps in services,
- Instituting changes in delivery system design based on the concept of a prepared care team and an activated patient,
- Documenting new design in job descriptions, orientation materials, flow diagrams, and organized charts,
- Providing staff with updates on delivery system design,
- Making Designated Staff Responsible for Follow-Up by Various Methods,
- Including Outreach Workers, Telephone Calls and Home Visits,
- Identifying follow-up needs, such as medication refills and symptom monitoring,
- Planning the follow-up approach, including who will contact patients, why, how, and when.

7:04:02- Roles, Duties and Responsibilities

This is very crucial in a hospital setting. Defining, specifying and assigning roles, duties, and responsibilities for all tasks within the delivery system helps and facilitate the implementation of tasks and this can be achieved through some strategy planning such as:
  *System Design, especially for planned visits to a Multidisciplinary Care Team:
  This involves determining who has responsibility for each step of the planned or acute visit and for follow-up, determining a timeline for tasks, training staff for new roles and responsibilities detailed in the new delivery

system design, obtaining senior leader support for training staff in new roles and tasks. This also involves identifying who will do the training, identifying resources, training material, and tools and using cross training to expand staff capability. The staff member being cross-trained should shadow or observe the staff member doing the procedure (e.g., Nurse Manager constraining with a Psychologist or Surgeon to learn how to conduct a brief depression screen.)

7:04:03- Assignment and Accountability

There is a general lack of accountability on the part of healthcare professionals in most African countries and this pertinent issue needs to be addressed at all levels. For an effective and efficient accountability system to be operational in a healthcare system, the following strategic steps should be established:

- Assign Accountability for Continued Clinical Improvement at All Levels of the Organization,
- Encourage the senior leaders to provide time for a day-to-day team leader to manage the initiative,
- Assign accountability for day-to-day leadership for continued clinical improvement,
- Ask the senior leader to identify an enthusiastic and respected clinician to champion the work and the team,
- Establish accountability of the clinical leaders for improvement activities. Ensure that clinical leaders develop improvement knowledge and skills,
- Ensure that the clinical leader reports to the staff and the center about improvement activities,
- Make leaders and the team accountable for improvement,
- Engage administrative and clinical staff in the improvement activities, so that people at all levels are aware of the beneficial changes,
- Regularly evaluate the team process as evidenced by regularly of meetings and reaching set goals,

7:04:04—Various Support Systems

Healthcare services in Africa require a lot of support systems for their sustainability in the market place and ultimate survival. Effective disease prevention programs use explicit, current guidelines or protocols. Reminders flow sheets/progress notes, provider education materials and sessions, appropriate input and collaborative support from relevant medical specialties, and patient participation are all part of a process to implement current guidelines in the clinical setting. Given the rapid changes in resistance patterns and other factors affecting the management of diseases, keeping updated on the most recent guidelines is especially important for providers caring for patients with this disease.

1) Community:

Linkages between health clinics and community resources such as AIDS service organizations, health departments, hospitals, churches, senior centers and schools are crucial to the success of HIV/AIDS and other health programs. Clinics form partnerships with community organizations to develop evidence-based programs, resources, and health policies that support patients in their efforts to live with HIV/AIDS disease. Clinics with strong linkages to the community make special efforts to coordinate care guidelines, measures, and resources throughout the community. Clinics that make these important links to community resources improve patient care and outcomes, and enable communities and patients to take an active role in managing a chronic illness, such as HIV/AIDS disease.

2) Delivery System Design:

Patients should be educated about the delivery system design by:

- Creating a patient orientation and self-management manual to teach patients about the new delivery system design,
- Ensuring that all new and existing patients are instructed about how clinic visits will be scheduled and conducted,
- Teaching patients how and when to notify the clinic of urgent care needs,
- Displaying information regarding delivery system changes in a waiting room,
- Ensure that a social worker is available to patients at every clinic visit in person or by cell phone/pager,
- Assessing patient satisfaction scores and quality of care report cards. Keep a running tally of waiting time.

7:04:05- Clinical Data and Information System

Due to the fact that a lot of health services are now technology-oriented there is need for African governments to adjust to these changes in order to be competitive. But due to the lack of financial and material resources as well as technical know-how, they continue to lag behind in this area. To provide good care for people with chronic diseases, clinicians need access to timely, clinically relevant information about each patient in the practice, as well as the population of patients as a whole. Useful information includes the following:

- Patient contact information,
- Patient's medical history,
- Case management and social work updates.

Providers can use the registry to record critical elements of the care plan, produce quick care summaries at the time of the visit, and enter data to alter the care plan as needed. A patient registry is most useful when patient data are available to the provider at the point of the patient visit, when decision support is most needed. The registry can remind providers of needed services, represent feedback on clinic and provider performance, and serve as a source of up-to-date information for encounters. Health care teams can also use the registry to contact groups of patients with similar care needs and deliver planned care and educational sessions. Although the registry is an important component of the clinical information system, other elements, such as scheduling and email systems, also support the delivery of good care to patients with chronic conditions such as HIV/AIDS disease.

7:04:06- Collaboration and Integration

An Integrative Collaborative Models is very good for a multidisciplinary team in a healthcare facility. This is absolutely good for most African countries since they are going through a lot of transformation and receive a lot of aid from international humanitarian organizations. The system should be designed to:

- Educate entire staff about the Care Model and the Model for Improvement,
- Using the data generated regarding improvements to enhance the image of the health center or clinic in the eyes of both internal and external leaders,
- Making quality part of everyone's job,
- Incorporating quality-related tasks in job descriptions,
- Articulating quality-related tasks in policies and procedures,
- Make the models the basis for all quality efforts,
- Adapting the models to the philosophy, goals and objectives of the organization.

CHAPTER EIGHT

8:00- TOTAL QUALITY MANAGEMENT IMPLEMENTATION PLAN

This is a strategic plan designed for an effective and efficient implementation of health services in ministries of health and their related departments and divisions, public and private health organizations, hospitals, clinics, health centers, health insurance companies, nursing and rehabilitation centers. This implementation plan is also beneficial to small and large-scale businesses, agro-industrial complexes, pharmaceutical industries and a host of other businesses needing quality in their products and services as well as their overall operation. The healthcare industry in Africa definitely needs a strategic Total Quality Management implementation plan of this nature in order fro it to be competitive and be able to sustain itself for the next century. This plan contain seventeen important implementation steps which include top management commitment, development of a corporate strategic plan, development of an organizational structure, development of an implementation budget, creation of quality council, teams and panels, starting an awareness plan, training of team leaders and facilitators, conduction of an initial survey, documentation of the implementation plan, quality system documentation, documentation control, actual implementation, internal quality audit, management review, pre-assessment audit, certification and registration and continuous quality improvement.

The implementation of TQM affects the entire organization from the start and is pursued with total dedication because it will result in a "paradigm shift" and "cultural transition". The implementation process depends on the sophistication of the society and organization, the size of the organization and the complexity of the process. The basic elements of implementation planning include specifying program goals to be addressed in the identified time period, determining program logic, targeting specific audiences, specifying desired outcomes, determining the current situation, identifying sequenced learning strategies, determining resource needs, and selection of specific marketing, delivery, and evaluation methods. Some of the benefits of effective implementation planning include:

A)- Opportunities for increased program impact,
B)- Sequence and continuity in educational programs,
C)- Clarification of actions and resources needed to implement a program,
D)- planned program marketing,
E)- Improved evaluation and accountability,
F)- Improved scheduling and management of time and other resources, and
G)- Greater personal satisfaction through a sense of progress and accomplishment.

During the "Establishment Stage", there is planning for leadership training, formation of the executive council, formulation of the philosophy, formation of the quality council, development of the training plan and formation of the quality boards. During the implementation stage too, the assessment of systems occurs, data analysis is ongoing and intervention strategies are being tried. There is also the adoption of the process improvement method and the board and the quality departments begin to assist teams with tools and techniques on an ongoing basis.

The introduction and implementation of the Total Quality Management concept into the African Healthcare industry is of crucial importance since it will help to redress some of the catalogue of managerial, structural and organizational problems affecting the system. If this goal is realized, the health sector in Africa might improve on the quality of its services by up to 25%. A typical TQM project takes between 3–5 years to be fully implemented. But some of the positive effects and impact are being felt from the second year of implementation.

The implementation of the TQM plan in an organization requires some activities and processes to be carried out for an effective and efficient system operation. Some of these processes are top management commitment, corporate strategic plan, organizational structure, implementation budget, formation of team and panels, awareness programs, training, status surveys, documentation, control, quality audit, management review, certification, registration and continuous quality improvement.

8:01-TOP MANAGEMENT COMMITMENT

Top management notably the Minister of Health, the Medical officer, Hospital Administrator or the Chief Executive Officer of the medical facility should demonstrate a commitment and a determination to implement the Total Quality Management system in the organization. It should also be convinced that registration and certification will enable the organization to demonstrate to its customers a visible commitment to quality and that a quality management system would improve overall business efficiency by the elimination of wasteful duplication in management system.

Initially, an orientation is carried out by the Chief Executive Officer (CEO) for all staffs in the health service and conveys the rationale for TQM implementation. The basic principles and philosophies of this concept are introduced. This is because TQM is a "paradigm shift", involving a change in culture, thought process, ideas, work habits and professional relationships. This involves moving an organization from a traditional system of operation to a modern one.

Top management should: -

- Communicate the importance of meeting customer as well as statutory and regulatory requirements to the organization,
- Define the organization's quality policy and make it known to every employee,
- Ensure that quality objectives are established at all levels and functions,
- Ensure the availability of resources required for the development and implementation of the quality management system,
- Appoint a management representative to coordinate quality management system activities, and
- Conduct a management review.

Top management should identify goals to be achieved through the quality management system such as being more efficient and profitable, producing products and services that consistently meet customer's needs and expectations, achieving customer satisfaction, increasing market share, improving communication and morale in the organization, reducing costs and liabilities and increasing confidence in the production system.

8:02- DEVELOPMENT OF CORPORATE STRATEGIC PLAN

The African Healthcare industry requires a strategic plan for the implementation of the Total Quality Management concept. The corporate strategic plan is the "blue print" for the implementation of an organization's vision, goals and objectives, and other activities required fir an effective and efficient production and delivery of products and services. The process is strategic because it involves preparing the best way to respond to the circumstances of the organization's environment, whether or not its circumstances are known in advance;

nonprofits often must respond to dynamic and even hostile environments. Being strategic, then, means being clear about the organizations resources, and incorporating both into being consciously responsive to a dynamic environment.

The focus of the corporate strategic plan is on the following:

- Corporate Vision—what the organization wants to be, future products and services concepts and future markets.
- Corporate Mission—how to achieve the corporate vision within a certain time frame, activities to achieve the vision, understanding of top management to line workers, the public, customers and suppliers.

As with any management tool, the strategic plan is used to help an organization do a better job that is to focus its energy, to ensure that members of the organization are working toward the same goals, and to assess and adjust the organization's direction in response to a changing environment. In short, strategic planning is a disciplined effort to produce fundamental decisions and actions that shape and guide what an organization is, what is does, and why it does it, with a focus on the future.

The process is about planning because it involves intentionally setting goals (i.e., choosing a desired future) and developing an approach to achieving those goals. The process is disciplined in that it calls for a certain order and pattern to keep it focused and productive. The process raises a sequence of questions that helps planners examine experience, test assumptions, gather and incorporate information about the present, and anticipate the environment in which the organization will be working in the future. Finally, the process is about fundamental decisions and actions because choices must be made in order to answer the sequence of questions mentioned above. The plan is ultimately no more, and no less, than a set of decisions about what to do, why to do it, and how to do it. Because it is impossible to do everything that needs to be done in the world, strategic planning implies that some organizational decisions and actions are more important than others—and that much of the strategy lies in making the tough decisions about what is most important to achieving the organizational success.

The strategic planning can be complex, challenging and even messy, but it always defined by the basic ideas outlined above—and you can always return to these basics for insight into your own strategic planning process.

1) Strategic Planning and Long-Range Planning:

Although many use these terms interchangeably, strategic planning and long-range planning differ in their emphasis on the "assumed" environment. Long-range planning is generally considered to mean the development of a plan for accomplishing a goal or set of goals over a period of several years, with the assumption that current knowledge about future conditions is sufficiently reliable to ensure the plan's reliability over the duration of its implementation. In the late fifties and early sixties, for example, the U.S. economy was relatively stable and somewhat predictable, and, therefore, long-range planning was both fashionable and useful.

On the other hand, strategic planning assumes that an organization must be responsive to a dynamic, changing environment (not the more stable environment assumed for long-range planning). Certainly a common assumption has emerged in the nonprofit sector that the environment is indeed changeable, often in unpredictable ways. Strategic planning, then stresses the importance of making decisions that will ensure the organization's ability to successfully respond to changes in the environment.

Strategic planning is only useful if it supports strategic thinking and leads to strategic management-the basis for an effective organization. It means making that assessment using three key requirements about strategic thinking: a definite purpose can be in mind; an understanding of the environment, particularly of the forces that affect or impede the fulfillment of that purpose; and creatively in developing effective responses to those forces. It follows, then that strategic management is the application of strategic thinking to the job of leading an organization and this entails attention to the "big picture" and the willingness to adapt to changing circumstances, and consists of the following three elements:

- Formulation of the organization's future mission in light of changing external factors such as regulation, competition, technology, and customers
- Development of a competitive strategy to achieve the mission
- Creation of an organizational structure, which will deploy resources to successfully carry out its competitive strategy.

2) Strategic Planning Model:

Many books and articles describe how best to do strategic planning, and many go to much greater lengths than this planning response sheet, but our purpose here is to present the fundamental steps that must be taken in the strategic planning process. Below is a brief description of the five steps in the process. These steps are a recommendation, but not the only recipe for creating a strategic plan; other sources may recommend entirely different steps or variations of these steps. However, the steps outlined below describe the basic work that needs to be done and the typical products of the process.

3) Getting Set for Implementation:

To get ready for strategic planning, an organization must first assess if it is ready. While a number of issues must be addressed in assessing readiness, the determination essentially comes down to whether an organization's leaders are truly committed to the effort, and whether they are able to devote the necessary attention to the "big picture". An organization that determines it is indeed ready to begin strategic planning must perform five tasks to pave the way for an organized process:

Identify specific issues or choices that the planning process should address
Clarify roles (who does what in the process)
Create a planning committee
Develop an organizational profile
Identify the information that must be collected to help make sound decisions.

4) Articulating Mission and Vision:

A mission statement is like an introductory paragraph: it lets the reader know where the writer is going, and it also shows that the write knows where he or she is going. Likewise, a mission statement must communicate the essence of an organization to the reader. An organization's ability to articulate its mission indicates its focus and purposefulness. A mission statement typically describes an organization in terms of its:

a) Purpose—why the organization exists, and what it seeks to accomplish,
b) Business—the main method or activity through which the organization tries it fulfill this purpose,
c) Values—the principles or beliefs that guide an organization's members as they pursue the organization's purpose.

Whereas the mission statement summarizes the what, how, and why of an organization's work, a vision statement presents an image of what success will look like. With mission and vision statements in hand, an organization has taken an important step towards creating a shared, coherent idea of what it is strategically planned for.

5) Assessment of the Situation:

Once a health service has committed to why it exists and what it does, it must take a clear-eyed look at its current situation. Remember, that part of strategic planning, thinking, and management is an awareness of resources and an eye to the future environment, so that an organization can successfully respond to changes in the environment. Situation assessment therefore means obtaining current information about the organizations strengths, weaknesses, and performance. - Information that will highlight the critical issues that the organization faces and that its strategic plan must address. The Planning Committee should agree on no more than five or to ten critical issues around which to organize the strategic plan.

6) Developing Strategies, Goals, and Objectives:

Once an organization's mission has been affirmed and its critical issues identified, it is time to figure out what to do about them:

a) The broad approaches to be taken (strategies) and
b) The general and specific results to be sought (the goals and objectives). Strategies, goals, and objectives may come from individual inspiration, group discussion, formal decision-making techniques, and so on—but the bottom line is that, in the end, the leadership agrees on how to address the critical issues. Discussions at this stage frequently will require additional information or a reevaluation of conclusions reached during the situation assessment. It is even possible that new insights will emerge which changes the thrust of the mission statement.

7) Completion of the Written Plan:

The mission has been articulated, the critical issues identified, and the goals and strategies agreed upon. This step essentially involves putting all that down on paper. Usually one member of the Planning Committee, the executive director, or even a planning consultant will draft a final planning document and submit it for review to all key decision makers (usually the board and senior staff). This is also the time to consult with senior staff to determine whether the document can be translated into operating plans (the subsequent detailed action plans for accomplishing the goals proposed by the strategic plan) and to ensure that the plan answers key questions about priorities and directions in sufficient detail to serve as a guide.

8:03- DEVELOPMENT OF AN ORGANIZATIONAL STRUCTURE

A preliminary step in TQM implementation is to assess the organization's current reality. This 'reality check' enables the organization's top management to identify the relevant preconditions to be done with the history; current needs, precipitating events leading to TQM and existing employee quality of life. The force field analysis helps in looking at which forces may be strengthened and which restraining forces may be eliminated, mitigated or counteracted. The organization should be healthy with determining factors such as available funds, strong administrative system, good managerial skills and high employee morale.

Desirable preconditions for an effective TQM implementation are identified in two areas: macro and micro. Macro factors include those, which are concerned with issues such as leadership, resources and surrounding infrastructure. The leadership should champion new ideas, there should be continuity of political leadership, a healthy civic infrastructure, shared vision and goals by leaders, trust among those in power, available outside resources and models to follow. The micro factors should center on top management support, customer focus, long-term strategic plans, employee recognition and training, employee empowerment and teamwork, measurement and analysis of products and processes and quality assurance.

In health and human services especially in hospitals and clinics, TQM changes the way clients are processed, the service delivery methods applied to them and ancillary organizational processes such as paperwork and procurement procedures. It changes its norms, values and systems and how it functions. It also changes the organization's political system-decision making processes and power bases. Information systems will be redesigned to measure and track new indicators such as service quality. Financial management processes may also need attention through the realignment of budgeting and resource allocation systems. A typical quality organizational structure is often mixed between a functional, project and matrix organizational structures. Various functional departments exist as specialized panels and are horizontally followed by quality improvement teams. Meanwhile outside consultants and mentors interact directly with the executive director, the quality council and the division of quality and planning. A typical quality organizational structure in a health service organization should comprise:

• The Executive Director (The Hospital Administrator)
• The Quality Council
• Quality Management Consultants and Contractors
• Specialized Panels representing various departments and divisions
• Quality Improvement Teams representing various departments
• Division of Quality and Planning
• Departments-Ongoing monitoring and evaluation.

A good healthcare system in Africa should have an organizational structure, which should enable it to better deliver quality effective and efficient services to clients. The organizational description below with various departments, divisions and units is a classic example for implementation as outlined below:

8:03:01-Health Information and Policy Departmen

Functions: Coordination and implementation of health plans, coordination and implementation of IT systems, public health information network, workforce development, epidemiology.

Divisions: This department has the following divisions:

State Registry and Vital Records:
Registration and statistics
Customer service and record search
Special records/Historical Preservation

Population Health:
Analysis, Reports, and Record Linking
Demographic Information
Family Health Surveys
Statistical and Methodological Consultation

Healthcare Information:
Physician Office Visits Data
Workforce Surveys
Health Institution Surveys
Board on healthcare Information
Institutional Review Board

8:03:02-Community Health Promotion Departmenty

Function: Media campaign, education and sensitization

Divisions: This department has the following divisions
A)- Family Health
Women's Health Program
Reproductive Health
Maternal/Prenatal health
Infant/Young Child Health
Adolescent Health
Birth defects Surveillance
Congenital Disorders
Genetics
Organ Donor Program
Injury prevention
Emergency Medical Services
Sexual health

B)- Public Health Nutrition and Physical Activity
Breastfeeding
Community Supplemental food Program

C)- Chronic Disease Division
Diabetic Prevention and Control Program
Arthritis Control Program
Cardiovascular Disease Program
Prostrate Cancer Program

8:03:03-Environmental and Occupational Health Department

Function: Lead Property Registration, Adult and Children Lead Poisoning
prevention, Lead and Asbestos Testing and Certification.

Divisions: This department has the following divisions
Food Safety and Recreational License
Restaurant, Lodging and Recreational Facility Licensing
Sanitation Regulation
Food Manager Certification

B)- Health Hazard Evaluation
Hazardous Wastes Sites Assessment
Health Hazard Investigation
Indoor Air Quality
Toxicology
Groundwater Standards
Occupational Health Hazard Prevention
Environmental Health Tracking
Asthma Intervention

C)- Radiation Protection
Radiological Emergency Response
Radioactive Material Program
Radiation Monitoring
X-Ray Registration
Mammography Quality Assurance

8:03:04-Communicable Disease Department

Functions: Counseling and Testing, Early Intervention, Insurance Coverage,
HIV/AIDS Prevention, Social Work and Case Management, Referrals.

Divisions: This department has the following divisions

A)- Immunization
Immunization Registry
Vaccination for Children
Hepatitis B
Adult Immunization
School Immunization
Vaccine purchase and distribution
Disease Surveillance
Education, Consultation, Technical Assistance

Communicable Disease and Epidemiology
TB Elimination
Anti-TB Medication Program
Infection Control
Hepatitis A
Food/Waterborne outbreaks
Public Health Veterinary
Influenza Surveillance
Outbreak Investigation
Laboratory and Hygiene Liaison
Sexually Transmitted Diseases
Surveillance/Epidemiology
Consultation/Technical Assistance
Prevention
Education
Syphilis Elimination

8:03:05-Emergency Medical Service Department

Functions: Paramedics, Ambulance, and First Aid

8:04- DEVELOPMENT OF IMPLEMENTATION BUDGET

The implementation and training plans for healthcare professionals in Africa (doctors, nurses, paramedics etc) must have cost related factors. Typical cost considerations are orientation, leadership training, train-the-trainer for selected staffs, facilitator training for selected staffs, off site training for the executive council, off site training for the quality department, general staff training, library materials, training aids and resources, facility costs and consultation. A good budget ensures the sustainability of any good healthcare delivery system.

8:05- QUALITY COUNCIL, TEAMS AND PANELS

The Quality Council consists of the Executive Director or Hospital Administrator, Senior Managers and Directors of the functional departments and divisions. The purpose of this is to manage team and departmental processes as well as results, focus on "how' rather than "who", use team approach to determine decision procedures, base team efforts on solid foundation of data, give responsibilities and accountabilities to team members, measure and monitor team goals and objectives, participate in meetings to achieve organizational goals, evaluate the effectiveness of meetings and develop agenda with team expectations and outcomes. Team and Panel members should include representatives of all units and departments of the organization—Marketing, Planning, Human Resources, Quality Improvement, and Public Relations/Customer Service, Hospital and Ancillary Operations, Financial services, Environmental Services etc.

8:06- STARTING AN AWARENESS PROGRAM

The TQM awareness program is conducted to communicate to employees the aims of the management system, the advantages to employees, customers and the organization, how it will work and their roles and responsibilities in the system. The program should stress the higher levels of participation and self-direction that the quality management system renders to employees. This is especially very vital for African hospitals and health ministries where extensive campaigns are needed for immunization and education of vast population on certain illnesses and epidemics.

8:07- TRAINING OF TEAM LEADERS AND FACILITATORS

One of the greatest problems of the African healthcare industry is the lack of qualitative in-service training. All healthcare professionals need to have ongoing training on various changes and technologies affecting health services in general as well as various techniques, strategies and ethical issues affecting the way they carry out their duties. This training emphasizes the importance of personal and team effectiveness and covers the basic concepts of quality management systems and the standards and their overall impact on the strategic goals and vision of the organization, the changed processes, and the likely work culture implications in the system. Initial training is also required for writing quality manuals, procedures and work instructions, auditing principles, techniques of laboratory management, calibration, testing procedures etc. It takes the individual from dependence to interdependence. Selected staffs are chosen as formal trainers and receive "training of trainers" instruction to edify their understanding of the material and to strengthen their teaching skills. Selected staffs are also chosen as "facilitators" because effective facilitation is integral to team processes to be used widely throughout the organization.

8:08- CONDUCTION AN INITIAL STATUS SURVEY

This involves comparing the existing quality management system in the health service with the Total Quality Management standard. A "gap analysis" is conducted whereby an organizational flow chart on process development and improvement is established, and documents requiring modification and elaboration should be identified and listed. During this review process, wide consultation with executives and representatives of various departments and divisions is required to enlist their cooperation. Resource people are identified for information gathering and a fairly organized and successful department is selected in order to develop the new system. Once it is approved, it is adapted, supplemented and implemented according to TQM standards. This often requires organizational arrangements, the drawing up of additional documents and possible removal of existing documents (e.g. procedures, inspection/test plans, inspection/test instructions) and records (e.g. inspection/test reports, inspection/test certificates).

8:09- DOCUMENTED IMPLEMENTATION PLAN

Once the organization has obtained a clear picture of how its quality management system compares to the TQM standard, all non-conformances must be addressed with a documented implementation plan. Usually the plan calls for identifying and describing processes to make the organization's quality management system fully in compliance with the standard. This involves the quality documentation to be developed, objectives of the system, person or team responsible, approval required, training required, resources required and estimated completion date. All these elements are organized in a detailed flow chart and each plan defining the responsibilities of various departments and personnel and setting target dates for the completion of activities.

8:10:00- QUALITY SYSTEM DOCUMENTATION

Documentation is very crucial for all medical services because if a service is not documented, then it was not rendered. It helps to protect healthcare professional in case of any eventuality. In the implementation of a Total Quality Management strategy, documentation of the quality management system should include documented statements of a quality policy and quality objectives, a quality manual, documented procedures and records required by the standard TQM, as well as documents needed by the organization to ensure the effective planning, operation and control of its processes.

8:11- DOCUMENT CONTROL

A documented system must be created to control the quality management system generated. This helps to manage the creation, approval, distribution, revision, storage and disposal of the various types of documentation. Document control should include:

• Approval for adequacy by authorized persons before issue,
• Review, updating and re-approval of documents by authorized persons,
• Identification of changes and the revision status of the documents,
• Availability of relevant versions of documents at point of use,
• Identification and control of documents of external origin,
• Assurance of legibility and identifiably of documents, and
• Prevention of unintended use of obsolete documents.

The principle of TQM document control is that employees should have access to the documentation and records needed to fulfill their responsibilities.

8:12- IMPLEMENTATION

The implementation process of the Total Quality Management strategy in any healthcare service should be monitored to ensure that the quality management system is effective and efficient and conforms to the standard. These activities include internal quality audits, formal corrective action and management review. It is also advisable to evaluate areas where the chances of a positive evaluation are high, to maintain the confidence of both management and staff on the merits of implementing the quality management system.

8:13- INTERNAL QUALITY AUDIT

The effectiveness of the system should be checked by regular internal quality audits as the system is being installed. This helps to verify that the installed management system conforms to the planned arrangements, to the requirements of the TQM standard and to the quality management system established by the organization. This is also to ensure that it is effectively implemented and maintained, and should be planned and performed as part of the ongoing strategy.

8:14-MANAGEMENT REVIEW

This is an activity often carried out by the Health Service Administrator. An internal audit and management review should be conducted and corrective actions implemented when the installed quality management system has been operating from three to six months. The management reviews are conducted to ensure the continuing stability, suitability, adequacy and effectiveness of the quality management system. The review includes assessing opportunities for improvement and the need for changes to the quality management system, including the quality policy and quality objectives. The input to management review should include information on results of audits, customer feed back, process performance, product conformity, status of preventive and corrective actions, follow-up actions from previous management reviews, changes that could affect the quality management system and recommendations for improvements. Management reviews should also address the pitfalls to effective implementation, lack of executive commitment, failure to involve everyone in the process and the failure to monitor progress and enforce deadlines.

8:15- PRE-ASSESSMENT AUDIT

The pre-assessment audit provides a degree of confidence for formally going ahead with an application for certification as a quality management organization. Normally an independent and qualified auditor is hired for the pre-assessment before applying for certification.

8:16- CERTIFICATION AND REGISTRATION

Once the quality management system has been in operation for a few months and has stabilized, a formal application for certification is made to a certification agency. If the documents conform to the requirements of the quality standard, the on-site audit is carried out. If the certification body finds the system to be working satisfactorily, it awards the organization a certificate of operation for a period of three years. During this period, it will carry out

periodic surveillance audits to ensure that the system is continuing to operate satisfactorily.

8:17- CONTINUOUS QUALITY IMPROVEMENT (CQI)

Certification to Total Quality Management standards in any health service in
Africa is not an end. The institution should continually seek to improve the
effectiveness and suitability of the quality management system through the
use of quality policy, quality objectives, audit results, analysis of data, corrective and preventive actions and management reviews. This is extremely
important to hospitals and clinics. The basic concepts behind Continuous
Quality Improvement are:

1) Quality in Fact:
   • Doing the right thing,
   • Doing it the right way,
   • Doing it right the first time,
   • Doing it on time.

2) Quality in Perception:
   • Delivering the right product or service,
   • Satisfying customer's needs,
   • Meeting customer's expectations,
   • Treating customers with dignity, integrity, courtesy and respect.

3) Measurement of Quality:
   • Accuracy—whether the target diagnosis or range is hit,
   • Precision—how well a procedure produces a value,
   • Data plotting techniques (statistical graphs),
   • Charts (flow, control, Pareto, histogram, run scatter, pie).

4) Benchmarks of Quality:
   • Organization's own standards,
   • Utilization Reviews,
   • Institutional Standards (eg. Critical Care Pathways),
   • Peer Review/Professional Standards,
   • Country Regulations for example Inspections, Proficiency Surveys etc.

5) Quality Control:
   • Monitoring elements of care eg. Instruments and test procedures,
   • Testing systems monitored so that the test results are valid,
   • Statistics validating test results,
   • Focus on performance not test utility,

- Problem-focused not patient-focused,
- Seeks random improvement rather than systematic improvement,
- Follow organizational workflow charts.

6) Quality Assurance:
  - Activities directed towards assuring quality of products and services,
  - Identification of important aspects of care,
  - Establishment of thresholds or benchmarks (eg.100%),
  - Monitoring Performance,
  - Identification of Problems,
  - Correction of Problems,
  - Evaluation of Effectiveness of Systems (i.e., Continuous Monitoring).

The basic principle in CQI is to seek to increase probability of desired patient outcomes, assess and improve processes involved in patient care, that processes be carried out by all staffs, that people do unintentionally make mistakes and that undesirable patient outcomes can be avoided if processes are improved. The outstanding features of CQI are that it is proactive; process focused, follow functional lines (how patients move through the process), seeks continued improvement and requires responsibility of all employees (this necessitates team approach).

Conclusion

In contemporary business, it is unrealistic to talk about projects and program without an effective and efficient strategy to implement them; it is also unrealistic to talk about quality products and services without systems and structures in place to facilitate their production; and neither can we talk about management in an organization without the development of the human resource potential. All these aspects in an organization are interdependent and the symbiotic relationship between them has tremendous effects and impact on its objectives, goals, mission and philosophy.

The healthcare industry in Africa is a victim of a catalogue political, financial and economic mismanagement and the Total Quality Management strategy is the best solution to address this dilemma. The implementation of the Total Quality Management strategy in Africa's health care industry will yield qualitative service delivery and develop relationships and processes capable of generating and sustaining quality improvement now and in the future.

Appendix

GLOSSARY

Accountability- being answerable to one's superior in an organization for the exercise of one's authority and the performance of one's duties, being answerable for one's results.

Action Plan- A plans that describes what needs to be done and when it needs to be completed. It also a description of what needs to be done by who, when and how.

Administration- The aspect of the organization responsible for directing and managing the activities of the organization, program, project or major work packages.

Administrative Management- Management that operates in the public trust, such as national, regional or local government administrations. It is often designed to survive indefinitely and the intended goal is to provide an environment acceptable to its constituents for their survival, prosperity and comfort.

Analysis- The study and examination of something complex and separation into more simple components- causes, variances, effects and impact and corrective action.

Audit- A systematic examination of records and documents to determine adequacy and effectiveness in budgeting, accounting, financial and related policies and procedures.

Authority- The legitimate power given to a person in an organization to utilize the resources to reach an objective and to exercise discipline.

Baseline- a planning and control instrument in the form of a summary attributes such as quantity, quality, timing, costs, etc that establishes a formal reference for comparison and verification of subsequent efforts, progress, analysis and control.

Break-Even Point- the productivity point at which value earned equals total cost.

Bureaucracy- A centralized system of administration for the conduct of business in a given field, usually highly structured and constrained by regulations, protocol, policies and procedures, and consequently is slow to react to change.

Business Engineering- A set of techniques that a company uses to design its business according to specific goals.

***Business Reengineering*-** to perform business engineering where a comprehensive review of all business processes is undertaken in order to find completely new ways of restructuring them in order to achieve radical improvements.

***Communication*-** The transmission and validated receipt of information so that the recipient understands what the senders intends, and the sender assures that the intent is understood.

***Concept Study*-** Consideration of an idea that includes a review of its practicality, suitability, cost-effectiveness, etc. usually followed by a recommendation whether or not to proceed with the project.

***Configuration*-** The technical description needed to build, test, accept, operate, install, maintain and support a system

***Configuration Management*-** The process of designing, making and assembling the components of a project's deliverables in order to achieve the required functionality; the process of defining the configuration items in a system, controlling the release and change of those items throughout the project, recording and reporting the status of the configuration items and verifying their completeness. Its management process for establishing and maintaining consistency of a product or service performance, functional and physical attributes with its requirements, design and operational information throughout the process.

***Contingency Planning*-** The development of managerial plans to be invoked in the event of specific risk events or that use alternative strategies to ensure project success if specific risk events occur.

***Continuous Quality Improvement*-** This is doing the right thing, doing it the right way, doing it right the first time and doing it on time.

***Contract*-** A mutually binding agreement in which the contractor is obligated to provide services or products and the buyer is obligated to provide payment for them. Contracts fall into three categories: fixed price, cost reimbursable to unit price.

***Culture*-** a pattern of artifacts, behaviors, values, beliefs, and assumptions that a group develops as it learns to cope with internal and external problems of survival and prosperity.

***Development*-** The systematic use of scientific and technical knowledge in the design, development, test, and evaluation of a potential new product or service for the purpose of meeting specific performance requirements or objectives.

***Design*-** The process of developing and documenting a solution to a problem using technology experts and tools.

***Effectiveness*-** A measure of the quality of attainment in meeting the objectives, the extent to which the goals of a project are attained, or the degree to which a system can be expected to achieve a set of specific requirements.

***Efficiency*-** A measures, (expressed as a percentage) of how well a process functions. Efficiency is calculated by dividing the total time taken to complete a task by the product of the longest cycle time of the entire process and the number of workstation.

***Empowerment*-** the enabling of project team members to achieve self-control to do their jobs with minimum supervision and with individual capabilities.

***Entrepreneur*-** A person who has the ability to see an opportunity, to obtain necessary capital, labor, and other inputs, and to know how to together an operation successfully, who has the willingness to take personal risks of success or failure.

Feasibility- The assessment of capability of being completed: the possibility, probability and suitability of accomplishment.

Feasibility Study- the methods and techniques used to examine technical and cost data to determine the economic potential and the practicality of project applications. This involves the analysis of variables such as interest rates, present worth factors, capitalization costs, operating costs, depreciation etc.

Flow Chart- A graphic means of depicting the steps or activities that constitute a process, often constructed from standard symbols representing a process or activity, decision, terminal, document flow lines, connector and terminal.

Functional Organization- An organizational structure in which staffs are grouped hierarchically by specialty e.g., production, marketing, engineering, accounting etc.

General Manager- An executive level position responsible for integrating all project activities with the corporate strategic plan.

Goal- a statement of the strategic direction pursued by managers

Health Maintenance organization (HMO)- this is an entity with an organized system for providing health care in a geographic area, on an agreed set of basic and supplemental health maintenance and treatment services, voluntarily enrolls its members and is reimbursed for services through a pre-determined, fixed, periodic payment made.

Health System- An organization by which an individual or group's health is being managed for an effective and efficient service delivery.

Health Insurance- The method of payment of a person's health benefits.

Human Resources Management- The function of directing and coordinating human resources throughout the life of a project by applying the art and science of behavioral and administrative knowledge to achieve predetermined project objectives of scope, cost, time, quality and participant satisfaction.

Hypothesis- A supposition that is fully understood, that is not proven but assumed for purposes of argument.

Implementation- The part of the project life cycle during which working drawings, specifications, and contract documents are prepared and contracts are tendered and awarded and the actual work undertaken.

Implementation Planning- the process of converting all requirements into a logically sequenced set of project works authorizing agreements and subcontracts that define and authorize all work to be performed for the project.

Indicator- Information in a consistent format that points to a current status, trend or need for action.

Industrial Relations- An organizational function that deals with the relationships that exist between management personnel and the unions with organization.

Information Management- The management of the systems, activities, and data that allows information in a project to be effectively acquired, stored, processed, accessed, communicated and archived.

Information System- A combination of personnel, efforts, forms, instructions, procedures, data, communication facilities and equipment that provide and organized and interconnected means for displaying information in support of specific functions.

Information Systems- A structured, interacting, complex of persons, machines and procedures designed to produce information which is collected from both internal and external sources for use as a basis for decision-making in specific contract/procurement activities.

Information Technology- Interconnected systems and equipment used in automated acquisition, storage, manipulation, management, movement, control, display, switching, interchange, transmission, or reception of data or information.

ISO 900 series standards- A set of related international standards on quality management and quality assurance developed to help companies effectively document the quality system element to be implemented to maintain an efficient quality system in a project or operation. These standards, initially developed in 1987 are not specific to any particular industry, product or service. The International Organization developed the standards for Standardization (ISO), a specialized agency for standardization composed of national standards boards of over 91 countries.

Job Description- Written outline of skills, responsibilities, knowledge, authority, environment and interrelationships involved in an individual's job.

Key Performance Indicators- Project management factors that are determined at the beginning of the project, reflect on the key objectives of the project provide the basis for project management trade-off decisions, measurable to reflect the critical success factors of the project.

Law- A binding custom or practice of a community enforced by the judiciary, a rule of conduct or action prescribed or formally recognized as binding or enforced by a controlling authority.

Leadership- The ability to set goals and objectives and generating enthusiasm and motivation amongst project team members and stakeholders to work towards these objectives.

Logistics- The business of planning and carrying out the movement and maintenance of resources to accomplish a particular task.

Management- The process of planning, organizing, executing, coordinating, monitoring, forecasting and exercising control to make sure that results are obtained according to established performance standards for scope, quality, time and cost.

Management Information System- a system dedicated to increasing the effectiveness of the organization by implementing computer-based data retrieval, presentation systems and productivity tools.

Medicaid (USA)- Federal-state programs established under Title XIX of the Social Security Act that finance payments to providers of health care services for low-income persons eligible under the law.

Medicare (USA)- a national health insurance program, established under Title XVIII of the Social Security Act for people aged 65 and over, for persons who have been eligible for social security disability payments for at least two years, and for certain persons who need kidney transplantation or dialysis.

Mission- The fundamental purpose of an organization in terms of customer need, core product or service, target markets, and technology used to satisfy the need stated in a way that sets the organization apart from others of its type.

Monitoring- The act of overseeing the progress of a project or activity, and of ensuring that it is conducted, recorded and reported in conformity with the quality standards and protocol set.

Networking- The exchange of information or services among individuals, groups or organizations.

Objective- A quantified business or corporate level performance target to be reached in a specified time frame.

Operation- Work performed by people and machines on materials or information; it transforms input into output; includes operational tasks for doing the work and operational methods guiding the work.

Organization- A company, corporation, firm or enterprise whether incorporated or not, public or private.

Organizational Structure- A structure that defines the reporting relationships, processes, systems and procedures of a project.

Paradigm- The organizational realities such as values, beliefs, traditional practices, methods, tools, that make members of the social group construct to integrate the thoughts and actions of its members. It provides rules and standards of management practice, laws, theories, applications, and instrumentation.

Paradigm Shift- when many beliefs and actions change in concert within an organization.

Performance- A quantitative and qualitative measure characterizing a physical or functional attribute relating to the execution of an operation or function. Performance attributes include (how many or how much) quality, (how well) coverage (how much area, how far), timelines (how responsive, how frequent), and readiness (availability, mission/operational readiness). Performance is an attribute for all systems, people, products, services and processes including those for development, production, verification, deployment, operation, support, training and disposal. Thus supportability parameters, manufacturing process variability, reliability etc are all performance measures.

Policies- General statements or principles intended to guide individual thinking, decision-making and action.

Process- The flow of products, material, or information from one worker or operation to another to transport input into output for consumers: composed of four phenomena: - processing, inspection, transport and delay.

Problem Solving- Finding the cause of a problem and addressing the cause so that the problem does not return.

Protocol- A document that describes the objectives, design, methodology, statistical considerations and organization of a project.

Quality- a principle that encourages excellence in everything: - products, strategies, systems, processes and people. It advocates for accuracy, efficiency and effectiveness, appropriateness and patient satisfaction.

Quality Control- Activities directed towards monitoring instruments and test procedures, testing systems monitored so that the test results are valid and making sure that accurate statistics are used to validate results: the process of monitoring specific project results to determine if they comply with relevant standards and identifying ways to eliminate causes of unsatisfactory performance.

Quality Assurance- a program in which overall activities conducted are directed towards assuring quality of products and services provided: the development of a comprehensive program which includes the processes of identifying objectives and strategy, of client interaction and of organizing and coordinating planned and systematic controls for maintaining established standards.

Quality Audit- A systematic, independent examination and review to determine whether quality activities and related results comply with planned arrangements and whether these arrangements are implemented effectively and are suitable to achieve the objectives.

Research- Studious inquiry or examination, investigation or experimentation aimed at the discovery and interpretation of facts, or the revision of accepted theories or laws in the light of a fact.

Resource- any variable capable of definition that is required for the completion of an activity and may constrain the project. Resources can be people, equipment, facilities, funding or anything needed to perform work in a project.

System- this consists of an integrated collection of personnel, knowledge, abilities, motivation, equipment, machinery, methods, measures, processes, and task activities designed to achieve repetitive or reproducible results.

Strategy- The pattern of organizational moves and managerial approaches used to achieve organizational objectives and pursue the organizational mission.

Strategic Management- the process managers use to formulate and implement strategies for providing best customer value that will the objectives of the organization.

Syndrome- A group of related or coincident events, actions, or situations: a pattern of circumstances, signs, or indications, which characterize a particular social, economic or political condition.

Technology- The element of applied science needed for doing the to provide value in the goods and services produced: a manner of completing a task using technical processes, methods or knowledge.

Total Quality Management (TQM) - It is a people-focused management system that aims at continual increase in customer satisfaction at continually lowers real cost: a system for identifying what clients want, defining the organization's mission, measuring throughout the whole process how well performance meets the required standards and involving the total organization in the implementation of a deliberate policy of continuous improvement.

Unemployment Rate- The proportion of the workforce, which has either lost employment in the past month, or has active sought jobs unsuccessfully during that time.

Utility- The ability of a product to satisfy a consumer's needs.

Value Management- a structured means of improving effectiveness in line with the organization's goals. It refers to the overall process of identifying key issues and setting targets, identifying the teams and processes necessary to achieve these and implementing them to obtain positive results.

Value Management Study- a function-oriented appraisal of all elements of an item, system or process to achieve essential characteristics at minimum overall cost. This procedure involves information gathering, function analysis, creative solution generation, judgmental solution evaluation, development of alternatives, presentation of recommendations and approval, implementation of changes and follow-up reporting of results.

Work- The expenditure of effort, physical or mechanical in the cause of an activity or task: the performance of any service for which payment is to be made.

Total Quality Management Training Forms and Charts

1) DAILY ORGANIZER

DATE: / /

TIME	ACTIVITY	OUTCOME
6:00		
:30		
7:00		
:30		
8:00		
:30		
9:00		
:30		
10:00		
:30		
11:00		
:30		
12:00		
:30		
1:00		
:30		
2:00		
:30		
3:00		
:30		
4:00		
:30		
5:00		
:30		
6:00		
:30		
7:00		
:30		
8:00		
:30		
9:00		

2) WEEKLY ORGANIZER

WEEK ENDING:

DATE:

TIME	MONDAY	TUESDAY	WEDS.	THURS.	FRI	SAT	SUN
6:00							
:30							
7:00							
:30							
8:00							
:30							
9:00							
:30							
10:00							
:30							
11:00							
:30							
12:00							
:30							
1:00							
:30							
2:00							
:30							
3:00							
:30							
4:00							
:30							
5:00							
:30							
6:00							
:30							
7:00							
:30							
8:00							
:30							
9:00							

Appendix

3) MONTHLY ORGANIZER

MONTH OF

Day	MORNING	AFTERNOON	EVENING
1			
2			
3			
4			
5			
6			
7			
8			
9			
10			
11			
12			
13			
14			
15			
16			
17			
18			
19			
20			
21			
22			
23			
24			
25			
26			
27			
28			
29			
30			
31			
32			

COMMENTS:

4) CUSTOMER CONTACT SHEET

#	NAME	ADDRESS	PHONE	FAX	EMAIL
1					
2					
3					
4					
5					
6					
7					
8					
9					
10					
11					
12					
13					
14					

COMMENTS:

5) GOALS/OBJECTIVES SHEET

#	GOAL/OBJECTIVES	TIMEFRAME	ASSESSMENT	OUTCOME	NEXT PLAN
1					
2					
3					
4					
5					
6					
7					
8					
9					
10					
11					
12					
13					
14					

COMMENTS:

6) QUALITY IMPROVEMENT STRUCTURE:

<u>Organizational Leadership</u>

Executive

Quality Council

Quality Boards

<u>Process Leadership</u>

Improvement Teams

(Cross Functional)

(Departmental)

(Self-Directed)

<u>Project Leadership</u>

Work Groups

<u>Empowered Individuals</u>

Self-managed People

7) PROCESS IMPROVEMENT TEAMS:

CRITERIA	CROSS FUINCTIONAL	DEPARTMENTAL
Purpose	Improve processes spanning two or more departments	Improve operations within department
Size	5–8 members	7–10 members
Composition	Organization-wide representation	Department employees
Selection	Quality Council Priority first	Department Manager Team Managers
Accountable To	Quality Council	Department Manager
Average Life Cycle	1–24 meetings	Indefinite
Meeting Duration	1–2 hours	1–2 hours
Data Collection and Summarization	Team assignment Staff support	Team assignment Staff support
Implementation	Quality Council Department Managers	Department Managers Team Managers

8) ROLES AND RESPONSIBILITIES:

The neutral servants of the team are the Facilitator and Recorder. Both practice techniques to get the Team's picture, while staying out of the picture.

CRITERIA	FACILITATOR	RECORDER
Purpose	To promote effective group dynamics	Capture group memory
Major cencern	How decisions are made	How decisions are made
Principle responsibilities	Ensure equal participation by team members Mediate and resolve conflicts Provide feedback and support team leaders Suggest problem-solving techniques and tools Provide quality training No ownership in outcome	Record long-term and short-term group memory Instant record, easy reference Content, process recorded What, when, who captured Support facilitator No ownership in outcome
Position type	Organization-wide (Neutral)	Organization-wide (Neutral)
Selection	Personal characteristics	Technical capabilities

9) DEVELOPING Meeting Ground Rules:

ATTENDANCE
Who will schedule meeting, arrange for room, and notify members?
How will absences be handled?
Can team members be replaced for absenteeism?

TIME MANAGEMENT
How does the team define "on time"? Are starting and ending times enforced?
How will time allotted to agenda items be monitored?
What is the role of the timekeeper? Who will serve as timekeeper?

PARTICIPATION
What advance preparation is expected?
How will participation be monitored to ensure equal contributions?
How will activities be monitored to ensure productive meetings?
How are assignments made? What are the expectations for their completion?

COMMUNICATION
How did candid can members be? Is information confidential to team?
How will discussions be started? What if discussions get off track?
How will interruptions or side conversations be handled?
What listening skills are expected?
What forms of criticism are acceptable?
How will creativity be encouraged and negative thinking discouraged?

DECISION MAKING
How will differences of opinion be expressed and resolved?
How will conflicts among members be handled?
What process will be used to reach consensus? To guard against "group think"?
How will decisions be made?

DOCUMENTATION
What process will be used to set meeting agendas and allocate time?
How will agendas and minutes be distributed?
Who will serve as recorder of minutes?
Where will documentation be kept?

OTHER
What meeting interruptions are acceptable and non-acceptable?
How will breaks be handled?

10) MEETING GROUND RULES:

Team Name   Date

ATTENDANCE

TIME MANAGEMENT:

COMMUNICATION:

DECISION MAKING:

DOCUMENTATION:

OTHER:

11) DRAFTING A TEAM CHARTER

TEAM MISSION
What parts of the process or system should be studied?
What led to selection of this issue?
What data exists or is required to study the issue?

EXPECTED IMPROVEMENTS
What are the goals or expected outcomes of this study?
What magnitude of improvement is expected?
Who will approve and implement recommendations?

BOUNDARIES AND CONSTRAINTS
What parts of the process or system should not be studied?
What time or budgetary constraints are applicable?
What decision-making authority does the team have?

RESORUCES AVAILABLE
What internal or external experts should be consulted?
Who may be called upon to assist the team?
What support services are available such as computers, graphics, presentation materials, etc?
Who will cover for members during meetings?

TEAM REPRESENTATION
What functional areas will be represented?
What job titles members will represent?

12) TEAM CHARTER:

TEAM NAME   DATE

MISSION:

EXPECTED IMPROVEMENTS:

BOUNDARIES AND CONSTRAINTS:

RESOURCES AVAILABLE;

TEAM REPRESENTATION:

13) MEETING AGENDA: _____

_____ DATE: _____

STARTING TIME: ENDING TIME:

Agenda Item		Action Discussion	Person Responsible	Time Needed Information
1. Read Minutes from Previous Meeting.		I	Team	
2. Review Meeting Agenda		I, D	Team	
3.				
4				
5.				
6.				
7.				
8.				
9.				
10.				
11. Review Team processes Set agenda for next meeting		D	Team	

14) MINUTES RECORD

TEAM: _____ DATE: _____

STARTING TIME: _____ ENDING TIME; _____

Members Present
1.
2.
3.
4.
5.
6.
7.
8.

Key Discussion Points (attach documents as necessary)

Decisions and Action Items (attach documents as necessary)

Next steps

Next Meeting Date _____ Time _____ Place _____
Committed by _____   approved by _____

        Recorder   Team Leader

15) ATTENDANCE LOG:

TEAM: DATE TEAM CHARTERED:

Meeting Date

Member name

COMMENTS:

NEXT MEETING DATE:

16) TEAM PROJECT RECORD

Project Name   Date:

DESCRIPTION:

REASON FOR SELECTION (CURRENT STATE):

EXPECTED IMPROVEMENTS (FUTURE STATE):

PEOPLE/PROCESSES IMPACTED BY IMPLEMENTATION:

RESOURCES REQUIRED (PEOPLE, FINANCIAL, EQUIPMENT):

RESULTS:

TEAM REPRESENTATION:

PROJECT BEGAN: PROJECT ENDED   REPORTED BY

Bibliography

Kasmausk, Karen et al. IMPACT: *From the Frontiers of Global Health.* (1–8) National Geographic Society, 1145 17th Street, NW, Washington DC, 20036, USA, 2000.

Argenti, Paul A. *The Portable MBA Desk Reference: An Essential Business companion.* John Wiley & Sons Inc., 605 Third Avenue, New York, NY, 10158, USA, 1994. (134,135)

Greg Bounds ET. Al. *Beyond Total Quality Management: Toward the Emerging Paradigm.* McGraw-Hill Inc., New York, NY, USA, 1994.

Kushel, Gerald. *Reaching the Peak Performance Zone.* American Management Association, New York, USA, 1994.

Waitley, Denis. *Empires of the Mind: Lessons to Lead and Succeed in a Knowledge-based World.* William Morron and Company Inc. New York, NY, USA, 1995.

Bechtel, Michele L. *The Management Compass.* American Management Association, New York, NY, USA, 1995.

Weil, Thomas P. *Health Networks: Can they be the Solution?* The University of Michigan Press, Michigan, USA, 2001, (41–58; 100–123; 184–215; 241–299).

Seedhouse, David (Editor). *Reforming Healthcare: The Philosophy and the Practice of International Health Reform.* John Wiley & Sons Inc., 605 Third Ave., New York, NY, 10158, USA, 1995. (15–26; 101–120; 167–170).

Marshall, Edward M.D. *Transforming the Way We Work: The Power of the Collaborative Work Place.* American Management Association, New York, NY, 10087-7327, USA, 1995.

MacDonald, John. *Calling a Halt to Mindless Change: A Plea for Common Sense Management.* American Management Association International. New York, NY, 10087-7327, USA, 1997.

Drucker, Peter F. *Managing in Turbulent Times.* Harper & Row, Publishers, New York, NY, USA, 1980.

Meredith, Jack R. ET. Al. *Project Management. A Management Approach.* Second Edition. John Wiley & Sons, Inc. 605 Third Avenue, New York, NY, 10158, USA, 1985.

McReish, Kenneth Ed. *Guide to the Human Thought: Ideas that Shaped the World.* Bloomsbury Publishing Limited, London, UK, 1993.

Morfaw, John, N. *Fish Processing as an Income—Generating Activity among Women in Limbe,* Case Study Report. Pan-African Institute for Development, Buea, Cameron, West Africa, June 1989.

AllAfrica.com: Cameroon: Lack of Refresher Courses is a Problem, Cameron Tribune, September 23, 2004, http://allafrica.com/stories/200409230390.html

Quality Assurance Project. Healthcare and Workforce Improvement, http://www.qaproject.org/world/worldafrica.html

Advance Africa. Strengthening Management Capacity, http://www.advanceafrica.org/what_we_do/strengthening_management_Capacity/index.html

The Reading room. Performance Improvement Case Studies; Family Health and AIDS Prevention Project (SFPS), http://www.reproline.jhu.edu/english/6read/6pi/case/case_wa.html

Africa; JHPIEGO Corporation. Training in Reproductive Health, http://www.jhpiego.org/about/africa.html

The Council for Health Service Accreditation of Southern Africa (COHSASA). CHSASA Standards, http://www.chsasa.co.za/html/whatischsasa/standards.html

Wordiq.com. Healthcare System, http://www.wordiq.com/definition/Healthcare_system

Traditional African Medicine Conference. AFRICAN HEALING WISDOM: From Traditional to Current Applications and Research, Washington DC, Febuary 2005, http://www.procultura.org/AFRICA.html

Gigley-Kitchin, Virginia. BBC News/AFRICA/UN tackles African brain drain http://news.bbc.co.uk/1/hi/world/africa/652801.stm

Johnson, David. Africa's Brain Drain Slows Development: AFRICANA, Gateway to the Black World. http://www.africana.com/articles/daily/index_20000302.asp

The New York Times. Africa's Health-Care Brain Drain, August 13, 2004 http://www.nytimes.com/2004/08/13/opinion/13fri3.htm

WHO: Health service delivery; Introduction to quality assurance and accreditation of health services. WHO: Department of Health Service Provision, July 2000. http://www.who.int/health-services-delivery/performance/accreditation/

Quality Leadership Training. Shawnee Hills MH/MR Center, West Virginia, February 1993

The Population Council-Sub-Saharan Africa Region 2003 http://www.popcouncil.org/africa/africa.html

TQM: Total Quality Management Diagnostics. http://www.skyenet.net/~leg/tqm.htm

Center for African Family Studies. Building Africa's Capabilities for Healthier Families. http://www.cafs.org/about1.html

USAID in Africa-Health and Family Planning. http://www.usaid.gov/regions/afr/hlthfp.htnl

The African Medical and Research Foundation (AMREF) http://www.amref.org/whatisamref.htm

Ward, William J., Jr. *Health Care Budgeting & Financial Management for Non-Financial Managers.* Auburn House, 88 Post Road West, Westport, Connecticut, 06881, USA, 1994 (page1–19, 247–248).

Sarabok, Karen. *Project Management 1: Planning and Scheduling.* Project Excel Corporation, Hummelstown, Pennsylvania, USA. (19880

Sarabok, Karen. *Project Management 11: Cost, Evaluation and Control.* Project Excel Corporation, Hummelstown, Pennsylvania, USA. (1988)

Wideman, Max. Wideman's Comparative Glossary of project Management Terms, v2.1, May 2001. www.pmforum.org/library/glossary/PMG_A00.htm

Overview of the ISO System, May 2005. www.iso.org/iso/en/aboutiso/introduction/index.html

Hansen, Dexter, A., Total Quality Management (TQM) Tutorial/Help Page (Overview). March 2005. www.home.att.net/~iso9k1/tqm.html

West African Doctors and Healthcare Professionals network-Features, 2003 www.wadn.org/xoops/modules/news2/article.php?storyid=19

African Population and Health Research Center, March 2004. www.aphrc.org/strategic plan/researchfocus.html

African Council for Sustainable Health Development, 2005. www.acoshed.net/progs/.htm

UNFPA State of the World Population, 2004 www.unfpa.org/swp/2004/english/ch4/index.htm

UNDP/ United Nations Development Program, 2005 www.undp.org

UNICEF- Communities and Families- Developing behaviors for HIV? AIDS prevention, 2005 www.unicef.org/communities/index_aids.html

Afro-Nets: African Networks fro Health Research and Development www.afronets.org/igha.php

Integrated Quality Diagnostics, Inc. TQM: The 9 TQM tools, The 9 TQM SPC Tools. www.iqd.com/pfttools.htm

Health System Trust: www.hst.org.za/generic/1

Motherland Nigeria: Healthcare; Current Health policy. www.motherlandnigeria.com/health.html\

Aga Khan Health Services- where Aga Khan Works. www.akdn.org/agency/akhswork.html

National Institute of Allergic and Infectious Diseases. NIAID: Sub-Saharan Africa. www.niaid.rti.org/index.cfm

INDEX

About the Author

Mr. John Ngosong Morfaw hails from Fonge Village, Lebialem Division in the Republic of Cameroon, West Africa. After his primary education at Sacred Heart School, Fiango-Kumba he went to Our Lady Seat of Wisdom College, Fontem (a catholic mission college operated by the Focolarini movement from Italy). Here he earned the nickname *"SIR JOHNNY MOR"* from his creative and other scholarly activities. He later completed high school at the Cameroon College of Arts and Sciences, CCAS, Kumba. With his high school Diploma the author taught briefly at the Vocational College of Arts, Muyuka, where he was the Head of the French Department, and later at the National Comprehensive College, Limbe, before proceeding to the National School of Social Affairs, ENAAS, Yaoundé. Upon graduation in 1985, he was posted to the Delegation in Buea where he represented the agency for the National Five Year Development Plan and was a Research Officer for the National Research on the Cameroonian Family in 1987. The author represented the agency at the provincial Radio Station in Buea as a Radio Talk Show Host in a program titled- "Social Welfare and the Society".

In 1988, Mr. Morfaw was admitted into the Pan-African Institute for Development in Buea where he proudly graduated with a Diploma in Project Planning and Management in 1989. In April 1990, he was awarded a scholarship as an Exchange Student to the USA through the Council of International Programs in Cleveland, Ohio. During the program he had orientation on American history, politics, social, cultural and academic policies at Cleveland State University. The author also took classes as a Graduate Audit Student at the Mandel School of Applied Social Sciences, Case Western Reserve University, Cleveland, Ohio.

The author moved to Pennsylvania and in 1995 he obtained a Bachelor Degree in Criminal Justice. He later graduated with a Maters of Science degree in

Administration from Lincoln University of the Commonwealth of Pennsylvania in 1999. In 2005 he was earned a Graduate Certificate in Project Management from the Graduate School of Professional Studies at Penn State University—Great Valley, Malvern, Pennsylvania, USA.

The author works as a Project Specialist with the Jewish Employment Services in Philadelphia, Pennsylvania and is involved with many community activities and organizations in various capacities. He is also the President and Chief Executive Officer of "Sir Johnny MOR Systems", an independent Project Management/Total Quality Management Consulting Firm. He is married to Pammy Asangong Mor, a Laboratory Scientist. They have two beautiful girls-Nkeng Mor and Muyang MOR, best known as the *"THE MOR SIS-TERS"*.